To Queenie J,

I love you.

Am so happy for
you and your
husband to have
found one another.

Together in faith
nothing shall be
impossible.

Love
Mary Fran

Walking Through a Miracle

ONE WOMAN…
ONE DAUGHTER…
ONE GOD…
AND A MIRACULOUS RECOVERY
FROM A LIFE-THREATENING COMA

Walking Through a Miracle

One Woman…
One Daughter…
One God…
And a Miraculous Recovery
From a Life-Threatening Coma

by Mary Frances Varallo

Harrison House
Tulsa, Oklahoma

Unless otherwise indicated, all Scripture quotations are taken from the *King James Version* of the Bible.

05 04 03 02 01   10 09 08 07 06 05 04 03 02 01

Walking Through a Miracle—
One Woman...One Daughter...One God...
And a Miraculous Recovery
From a Life-Threatening Coma
ISBN 1-57794-209-4
Copyright © 2001 by Mary Frances Varallo
P. O. Box 16
Nashville, Tennessee 37203

Published by Harrison House, Inc.
P. O. Box 35035
Tulsa, Oklahoma 74153

I dedicate this book to my husband, Dr. Nicholas Frank Varallo Jr., who, next to the Holy Spirit, is the most important and influential person in my life.

Nick, your unqualified love, friendship, and support have made me who I am today. Without you, I would have no ministry.

Your wisdom, strength, and protective concern are the earthly personification of the Father God. Your heart toward me and toward our family reveals God's love in ways I never dreamed. Thank you for being such a wonderful husband and father, and my dearest earthly friend.

Through the years, your insight, stability, and encouragement have walked me through many miracles. I respect and rely upon you so much. You are the finest man I know, and the only one I would ever want to share my life with.

I love you forever, Nicky.

Acknowledgments

To acknowledge by name everyone who walked through this miracle with us is impossible, if only for concern of omissions. It is important, however, for me to express my heartfelt thanks, at least in a general way.

If you are fortunate enough to be part of a close family that also lives in the same city, then you are truly blessed. Our wonderful son, Nicholas, my mom, Rita, and her husband, John Patton, my mother-in-law, "Nonie," my brother, Hal, and his wife, Margie, my sisters-in-law, Frances Ann and Aurelia, and Aurelia's husband, John, all put their lives on hold in order to help with the hundreds of details that seem so out of sync at a time like this. The same is true of aunts, uncles, and cousins who came from near and far to share their love and concern.

And oh so many friends came to our side. There were church friends, Christina's close friends and former classmates, Nicholas's friends, our best friends, our mutual friends, ministry friends, my ministry office staff, Nick's dental colleagues, his patients and office staff, and his golfing buddies. Some came early every morning, some every evening. Some came to pray, some to chat and tell tall tales to try to get our minds off the here and now. Some brought food; some traveled all the way to Houston. Some ran errands and did numerous favors. But above all else, they each brought an abundance of faith, hope, and love, and for that, we will be forever grateful.

Then there were the hundreds of medical personnel who became a part of our lives. The paramedics, the trauma ER staff, nurses, surgeons, and physicians of every sort, both in Nashville and in Houston, had their skills tested daily and even hourly in Christina's struggle for life. They are often unheralded but never unappreciated.

I must also thank the numerous ever patient therapists who were a constant part of Christina's life for many, many months.

Lastly, it is with a deep gratitude to Harrison House and staff, who so wanted this story told and offered to write and publish this book.

The writer, Andrell Stevens, has brought forth my heart-lived relationship with my "best friend," the Holy Spirit, God my Father, and my Savior and Lord, Jesus Christ. She interviewed me for endless hours, studied my tapes, and read what must have seemed like a million pages of transcriptions of my tapes and church services. We laughed and cried through the hours of sharing my life, my faith, and my beloved family.

Somehow she walked the corridors of my life and gathered the heralding moments to write this story. I believe she has done so in the excellency of the gift of God that she is unto the body of Christ. Thank you, thank you, my precious friend and sister in the Lord, Andrell Stevens, God's scribe.

Table of Contents

Foreword

Recently I spent an afternoon in front of a fire in my den with a copy of the manuscript for this book in my lap. Beginning with the very first chapter, I found myself attempting to read through tears as memories of those traumatic times in the life of Mary Frances, Christina, and the Varallo family came flooding back. It is not often one witnesses a miracle of this magnitude. It is even more rare to have the privilege of being a small part of it as I was with this one.

The Varallos have been a prominent family in our city for many years. They have successful businesses and professions and are energetically involved in the Nashville community. But it was not their prominence or successes or standing in the community that sustained them through the terrible events of this story. It was their relationship with their God. I am about to enter my twenty-fifth year of pastoring the local church my wife and I pioneered in this city. In that period of time, a pastor experiences much to rejoice over and much to weep over with many families. Through faith and patience we have seen many victories as well as some outcomes we would have desired to be different than they were. Christina's is one of the victories and by far the most miraculous.

When Mary Frances first came to my church over twenty years ago, she was a young Catholic housewife and mother of two young children. Coming to our church was a bold step requiring considerable courage. She came from the grand cathedrals of west Nashville to a little storefront church meeting in a former furniture store. She was there because her phenomenal relationship with the Father and His Son through the precious Holy Spirit had filled her with a hunger for God's Word, and she would not be denied. Sometimes we remember those days and laugh uproariously over how she used to call me Monsignor McRay. She knew very little about God's Word, but she did know God. I have preached for many years that one will not truly embrace the life-giving Word of God without having an intimate relationship with God. Mary Fran is one who has proven my case. Through her intimate relationship with her God, she embraced the Word like few people I have ever known. She grew spiritually by leaps and bounds. She spent countless hours in the Word and in prayer, both at home and in the church, all while at the same time being a responsible wife and mother. When she would encounter something in the Word or in prayer that she did not understand, she would come to me seeking answers. Fortunately I had a lot more time on my hands in those days, and we spent many hours over several years discussing a multitude of subjects in the Word of God. I knew then, of course, that this woman was not your ordinary housewife. God had a call on this woman's life that would impact both the church and the world.

I know with an absolute certainty that those years in the Word and in prayer and fellowship with the Father prepared the way for Mary Fran to walk through her miracle. Today Reverend Mary Frances Varallo, through her prophetic miracle-working ministry, is impacting multiple thousands of lives around the world. But the

Mary Fran you are about to meet in the pages of this
book was just a mom whose little girl was in big trouble.
But no matter how big the trouble, she knew her God
was much bigger. As you turn the following pages of
Walking Through a Miracle, you will become engrossed in
Christina's story. You will many times wipe away tears.
But in the end you will shout the Victory, for greater is He
that is in us than he that is in the world.

> Bill McRay
> Senior Pastor
> Victory Fellowship Church
> Nashville, Tennessee

Preface

I love the Holy Spirit. He has been so faithful and kind to me. A special place in my heart is reserved particularly for Him. I think such a place in the heart is always created for those with whom you spend much time. And so it is with me concerning the Holy Spirit, the Holy One. He is the One I know so well.

Most of us are comfortable with the Father and with the Son. But now, because of the time we have come into, it is important for each of us to also have a similar comfort zone with the Holy Spirit Whom the Father God has sent to teach and to guide us.

In closing his second letter to the Corinthian church, the apostle Paul committed them to the grace of the Lord

Jesus Christ, the love of God, and *the communion of the Holy Spirit. The Amplified Bible* translates that phrase as "the presence and fellowship (the communion and sharing together and participation) in the Holy Spirit." I like that.

You see, it is the Father's heart's desire for us, and the longing of His Spirit as well, that we enter into communion, or intimate fellowship, with the Holy Spirit—a fellowship of hearing and talking and laughing and crying with God, the Holy Spirit. That is how it is to be for all of us with the Holy Spirit. It was always meant to be that way. The Father and our Lord Jesus always intended for each of us to be ever so keenly aware of and comfortable with the Holy Spirit and with His voice, to understand what He does for us as sons of God in this time. He is here to help us overcome our humanity in order to do the will of God, just as He helped Jesus.

I am not a teacher. My part in this wonderful plan of God is not extraordinary or grand. My part is so simple. It is found in the simplicity of being the voice of one crying out: Come into the fellowship of God the Holy Spirit. Come now into the place of communion with Him reserved exclusively for you. He will teach you of the Father's love and the power in the name of Jesus.

Introduction

My family has experienced a magnificent and certifiably undisputed miracle from God. It is a most glorious testimony of Jesus Christ in a family's life. I want to share that experience with you because no matter what you may be facing in your life today, God wants you to know that He is willing to perform a miracle for you.

Just as surely as our family received life instead of death, mercy instead of judgment, and a mighty deliverance against all odds, God the Father wants to do the same thing for you.

However, it matters what you say about your situation.

God is a good God. He is a loving Father. You never have to be confused about what He wants. Unlike some people, God doesn't have mood swings. You can always know how God will act. You can always know what God will do. God is good—*all* the time. And He always, always, *always* looks out for your best interest.

Just as a good parent wants what is best for his or her child, God wants what is best for His children. For example, would good parents dangle food in front of their child and say, "See if you can reach the food," while at the same time making it as difficult as possible for the child to reach it?

We all know that a good, loving parent would never do that. But some people have the mistaken idea that God is like that. They think He is holding their miracle out just beyond their grasp so He can watch them struggle and strain, only to fall short of obtaining it. If good parents show their children the way to have success and then do all they can to help them obtain it, how much more will our faithful and loving Father God supply *all* that we need?

If you understand nothing else about God, at least understand this: God is a good God, and no good thing will He withhold from those who trust Him. You don't ever have to be confused about God. He is always the same. You can trust God to always, always, *always* look out for your best interest.

But you're never going to trust or have faith in anyone you don't know—not even God. Think about it. How did your best friend become your best friend? You spent time together, sharing your thoughts and feelings, until you knew that you could trust each other. To develop faith in God and a trusting fellowship with Him, you have to spend time with Him.

I'm not talking about just spending time reading your Bible. I'm talking about spending time communing with the Person of the Holy Spirit, developing an intimate friendship with Him. And the way to develop such a friendship with Him is to invite Him into every area of your life, practicing His presence in all you do and listening to His voice within your spirit.

When you're building a friendship, you don't do all the talking. There's some listening to be done. It's the same way when you cultivate a deeper fellowship with the Holy Spirit. There's some listening to be done. You need to listen as well as speak. And when you begin to expect God to speak to your heart, He will. Your anticipation is His invitation to come into your life. The Holy Spirit wants to so saturate you with Himself that your life becomes totally filled and flooded with Him.

That's what this book is about.

Do you need a miracle in your life? If so, I have good news for you: Our Father God has a miracle for you. He has made it easy for you to receive your miracle. Your miracle is near you. In fact, your miracle is in your mouth.

Jesus said, *"For verily I say unto you, That whosoever shall say unto this mountain, Be thou removed, and be thou cast into the sea; and shall not doubt in his heart, but shall believe that those things which he saith shall come to pass; he shall have whatsoever he saith"* (Mark 11:23).

I like knowing that I can have what I say. Don't you? The Creator of the universe, God Himself, said that if you believe something in your heart and then say what you believe with your own mouth, He will do it. That means, of course, anything that's in line with His will. *Anything* in line with God's will—and *God's Word* is *His will.*

22

Healing *is* God's will. Health *is* His will. God wants *you* well.

Our Father God paid a tremendous price for you and me to be free from sickness and disease. He gave us the ultimate, His highest and His best, to deliver us from the destruction of sin. He gave us His Word. He gave us His life. He gave us the blood of His own Son, Jesus Christ. And because of what Jesus accomplished for us on Calvary, we can be sure of this: healing belongs to us.

But healing does not always manifest immediately after you believe it and say it. What do you do then?

That's what this book is about.

I remember walking the long road to our miracle. At times along the way, I would get discouraged. I was doing all I knew to do, but nothing seemed to be happening. Nevertheless, I continued to hold on to the promise our Father God had made to me. I knew my Abba Father could not and would not lie to me. So I trusted Him. I believed and held on to His promises. I reminded Him of what He promised. And I waited.

Suddenly, the Father performed a glorious miracle in order to keep His promise to me.

Healing doesn't always manifest the moment you believe. But if you continue to believe God, healing *will* manifest. You have God's promise on it.

Our Father God made a promise to you in His Word that He will come through for you. I have watched Him do it for me, and I know He will do it for you. God is not a respecter of persons. He is a respecter of *faith*. When you release your faith through the words you speak, heaven *will* move on your behalf.

Are you in the middle of a battle that's been hard and long? Has the enemy hit you with an attack that seems impossible to overcome? Do you need a miracle? If you need a miracle, *you can have a miracle!* I know that is true because the Word of God declares it. All you need to do is unleash the miracle-working power of God by speaking His words into your situation. The Holy Spirit will even tell you which of His words to speak—that's how much He wants you to have your miracle!

Whoever you are, whatever your need may be, God loves you so much. God the Father gave you His Son to translate you out of darkness into the light. Then He sent you His Spirit to help you transform your circumstances and guide you through to victory. Now He has asked me to tell you how valuable you are and how much you mean to Him, and to let you know that if you need a miracle, you can have a miracle.

That's what this book is about...

Mary Frances Varallo

*...the presence and fellowship (the communion
and sharing together and participation)
in the Holy Spirit be with you all.*

2 CORINTHIANS 13:14 AMP

1

'Guide Me Through This, Holy Spirit'

"But if the Spirit of Him who raised Jesus from the dead dwells in you, He who raised Christ from the dead will also give life to your mortal bodies through His Spirit who dwells in you."

It seemed as if my heart were about to pound through my chest as I wove around and through the maze of wires, tubes, and machines pumping oxygen, fluid, and medication into various intensive-care patients. Hospital technicians scurried in and out of rooms and behind curtains, speaking quickly in muffled tones, doing all they could to keep several seriously ill or injured patients alive. Or, at least, comfortable.

Our own daughter, Christina, was among them.

Who could possibly imagine a day like the one our family just experienced?

A sickening feeling knotted my stomach as we made our way to her bedside. When I looked down at our daughter, I wanted to scream. Her face and body were terribly swollen, seemingly twice their normal size, and wires were protruding through her partially shaved skull. Surveying the tubes inserted into nearly every orifice of her body, I touched her blonde hair, matted with dried maroon-colored blood and splinters of debris which had gone unnoticed during the rapid flurry of more than twelve hours of emergency trauma surgery.

Dear God, could I have prayed differently to prevent this?

Earlier that morning during the height of Nashville's rush hour traffic, Christina had driven into the path of an oncoming truck. As her small Honda Civic hurled through the air, it cracked an electrical pole and slammed into a bridge abutment, landing as the pole crashed into the roof of her car. The violent impact rammed the car engine back through the dash into her chest and spun the car around, wrapping Christina within a cocoon of metal, wire, and glass. A ripped ear, torn aorta, ruptured spleen, fractured pelvis, broken hip, cracked ribs, broken arm and collarbone, and massive brain damage were among the many injuries she suffered.

The comatose young woman now lying before me was swollen and barely looked human, much less like our beautiful blonde, blue-eyed, twenty-three-year-old daughter. Softly I stroked Christina's bruised and swollen cheeks. Memories flowed in stream with the uncontrollable flood of tears pouring down my face.

Father, I trust You to guide me through this.

How could this have happened? Where was the open door that allowed this to occur? I didn't know the answers to those questions. I did know, however, that I couldn't afford such questions to be even a slight concern at this point. Too much was at stake to waste strength and dissipate faith with questions that might never be fully understood.

As soon as I learned of the accident, the Spirit of God promised life and wholeness for Christina. But that was *His* part to bring to pass. One question I did not dare to ignore was clear: What was *my* part to help us walk through this to a miracle?

Father God, I know You spoke to my heart life and wholeness for Christina. I don't know how You're going to do it, but I want You to know that I believe You will do this. But if You ask my opinion, I think right now would be a good time to do it!

Apparently, however, He wasn't asking for my opinion. He asked only for my trust.

I had no idea how long this journey would be, but I could tell it wasn't going to be an easy one. We were only a few hours into it, and already I was hit with more fear than I had ever battled in my entire life. Within a twelve-hour period, our daughter, Christina, had endured two major operations, including open-heart surgery. Doctors offered no hope of recovery. They were surprised she had survived this long. They certainly didn't expect her to live through the night.

With every new report, the prognosis grew bleaker. Would God be faithful to us in the midst of this? For me, that wasn't even a valid question. I knew God would be faithful to the end. The real question, however, was this: Would *I* believe Him and His words to me until the end—regardless of what I might hear or see?

A verse came to mind: *Abraham, being strong in faith, considered not his own body....* Yes, but it wasn't my body lying crushed and contorted into a near-fetal position. I wasn't the one with a hole drilled into my skull to monitor escalating pressure in the brain. If it were my body, it would have been easier to be like Abraham and not consider what can happen to a body, but it was *not* my body. It was *Christina's*—my only daughter, my precious child. I almost wished it could have been me lying there. I'd have traded places with my child in an instant in order to prevent her from having to go through this.

Dear God, how do I do this? I had learned so many lessons in trusting the faithfulness of God. Had I learned enough to get through this, to get our daughter through this? Was I really able to stand strong and trust Him when our daughter's very life depended upon it? Well, ready or not, I was about to find out.

Questions and Thoughts To Consider

Now, what I have to say may help you with some of the questions you are wondering about in your own life and situation. I believe that as you read my story, God will begin to speak to you about your own life. He will begin to show you the answers you have been waiting for. Please use the pages following each chapter to journal thoughts, questions, and revelations that come to you as you read.

Remember when I thought, *Dear God, could I have prayed differently to prevent this?* Perhaps you have asked yourself a similar question. Well, the answer to my question was this: If there had been another way to pray, the Holy Spirit would have told me.

And so it is for you. By His Spirit, God will guide you. He will counsel you. He will comfort you. He is not withholding the way of escape from you. He would never do that.

I understand the inner turmoil that can come when you're facing a situation that seems so far beyond your control. But know this: He will help you. Settle down your soul; calm your emotions; quiet your mind. Be still and listen on the inside to your own heart, to your own spirit. The Holy Spirit will speak to your spirit, not to your mind.

I'm not hearing anything, you may be thinking.

Well, then, do this: Pick up your Bible; then turn to the last five Psalms read them aloud and write your thoughts in the lines that follow. Why read the last five Psalms you ask? Because these Psalms are about Him, and when you are feeling anxious, you are too overwhelmed with "you" and your own situation. Your entire triune being—your spirit, soul, and body—will settle down as you hear yourself speak aloud of your compassionate, wonder-working, big God—and I do mean BIG! God is bigger than that which is trying to overwhelm you.

What are some situations you are going through that may seem trying right now? How is God showing you how to pray? After you've reviewed His direction in the matter, then pray with confidence knowing that His compassion, wisdom, and strength will lead you!

Journal

2

That I May Know Him

"For I am the Lord, I change not."

MALACHI 3:6

As I looked at Christina during this dark moment of her life, I knew that I must grasp hold of God's truth to keep from drowning in despair. I needed to hold on to faith that was grounded to a firm foundation. I needed to *know* God's salvation was available for us. Grasping for a memory of hope, I remembered the woman who came into our yard and told me the story of the dogwood tree....

"May I tell the child the story of the dogwood tree?" she asked.

Clutching my mother's hand, I timidly looked up at this unknown woman who had ventured uninvited onto our property. George, our gardener, immediately thrust himself forward as a barrier between the stranger and my mom and me.

"What do you want?" he asked her brusquely.

The woman never flinched. Calmly, she repeated her question. "May I tell the child the story of the dogwood tree?" she asked, looking at me and lifting her hand toward the beautiful tree blossoms surrounding us.

I drew close to my mother. I was a sheltered six-year-old who wasn't accustomed to seeing strangers around. Our gardener looked to my mother for an approving nod or shake of the head to determine what he should do. My mother agreed, so George stepped aside to let the woman pass. She walked straight toward me and said, "Child, give me your left hand." I froze in terror at those words.

No. Not my hand, again... I thought.

I was a left-handed child. And, although being left-handed may not seem so significant today, in those years any child with a left-handed tendency was forced to become right-handed. In the Catholic schools I attended, the method the nuns usually employed to encourage such a change was to strike the hand with a ruler.

'Jesus, Does Your Hand Hurt? My Hand Hurts, Too'

Beginning in kindergarten, I received firm and frequent blows to my left hand in an attempt to make me right-handed. This happened repeatedly. In addition to that, I stammered with certain words. These two things, having my hand beaten daily because my natural left-handedness was considered wrong and often having difficulty speaking clearly, made me an outcast among the other children. I had begun to believe that more than just my left-handedness was wrong. I started to feel that *I was wrong* as a person. And because the religious atmosphere that surrounded me reinforced that belief, I assumed that God was angry and thought I was wrong as well.

So when this stranger asked specifically for my left hand, just as the nuns did again and again each day, it frightened me. But there was a gentle quality in the sound of this woman's voice. For some reason, I felt I would be safe. So I stretched out my left hand and she placed it gently around one of the blossoms on the beautiful dogwood tree in our yard.

While I fingered the soft petals, the woman told me the story of Jesus. She noted that the brown and red markings on the dogwood blossom represented the nail prints in Jesus' hands, but she made a point to say that He was no longer nailed to the cross. The kind stranger explained that each spring dogwood blossoms remind us that Jesus rose again and is alive forevermore. He is not hanging on a cross but is seated in heaven next to God the Father.

Hearing that was very significant for me, because every day at school we went to church and genuflected before a huge crucifix depicting Jesus on the cross. My eyes were always riveted to the nails in His hands, and I would think, *Jesus, does Your hand hurt? My hand hurts, too.*

But that day, as I held a tiny dogwood blossom in my hand, I learned that Jesus had been nailed to a cross to take away my sins, my sicknesses, and my pain. He was not dead but alive, and He wanted to make His home in my heart. Although my mother and the gardener could also hear her story, the woman spoke directly to me. She explained how to ask Jesus into my heart; then she left.

That night after my parents put me to bed and closed the door, I got up out of bed, went over to the window, sat on the window seat, and looked out the window that overlooked the dogwood tree. I looked out into the night sky and cried for God because He had His Son back. And then I did as the lady had instructed. I asked Jesus to come into my heart and be my Savior. I remember asking, "How do You fit in my heart?" I told Him that I would love Him forever, and at that moment, my room was filled with a brilliance of light. Though it was a frightening moment, it was but for a moment and then peace and love consumed the room and then me.

Crying for the Father Because of His Son

Then I considered how the Father must have felt when Jesus died for our sins, bearing the pain of our punishment and our sicknesses in His own body. Suddenly I was gripped with sadness and began to cry with huge sobs for the Father because His Son had to die. Looking out my window at the dogwood tree, which now held so much meaning for me, I thought, *The only thing worse than what Jesus felt was to be His Father and have to watch it all happen.* As I cried, I also began to pray specifically for people who needed to be healed. My prayers were the simple words of a stammering six-year-old moved by compassion flowing from the heart of Father God.

After that night, anytime I saw a sick or handicapped person, I would pray for him as soon as I was alone in my room. A wave of compassion to see others healed continually swept over my heart, reflecting (even then) an expression of the Father's compassion that I would carry all my life.

The simple yet awesome way God chose to draw me to Him that day changed my life completely, in one remarkable moment. On that day, an unknown woman obeyed His instructions to find a specific child, at a specific location, to hold the hand all others hit, and to tell that child that God wasn't angry with her but loved her very much. On that day, my heart was consumed with a yearning that has never diminished. It is a yearning to know Him intimately and to tell others that He loves them completely.

'No, My Child, This Is Not the Way for You'

At the age of sixteen, I received the call of God on my life. As a Catholic girl, I thought that meant I would need to go into the convent and become a nun. Anyone who knows me today laughs at the thought of me in a convent. I would have shown up late for Mass and lost things—it just wouldn't have worked!

But back then, I was very serious about wanting to consecrate my life totally to God. So I drove up to the convent and asked to speak with the Mother Superior. We went into her office to talk, and I found her to be kind and attentive. After listening to me pour out my heart about my love for God and my desire to become a nun, she said, "Oh, yes, you can come here, finish your education, and then we'll send you to college. It will work just fine, Mary Frances." Then, suddenly, she stopped and said, "Oh. No, my child. No, this isn't the way for you. But God will guide you."

I was startled by how suddenly she shifted from yes to no. Here I was attempting to follow the Lord as best I knew, but I was rejected—told that I was wrong for the part. An outcast again—or so it seemed.

I was baffled. I wanted to serve God, and becoming a nun was the only way I knew to do that. But now the door was shut.

God opens doors and He shuts doors. When He shuts a door, it is based on His loving, merciful provision just as when He opens a door. God is so kind and faithful to interrupt our little plans when they would lead us away from His higher plan for our lives. At that particular moment, I had no idea how absolutely led of the Holy Spirit the Mother Superior was to speak those words to me.

From that point on, I just did what I knew to do and trusted Him to guide me. I attended college and I married Nick Varallo, who was a graduate of Notre Dame, whom I had known (and had a crush on!) since high school. Nick was always a leader—so strong in character, and intellect, and polished in demeanor. He was, and is now even more so, ambassador-like in his ability to communicate with people, particularly in matters of business. He is gifted in bringing situations to a wise conclusion.

Nick completed dental school, and some time afterward, we eventually started our own family. I continued to love God and serve Him as best I knew how, although I really wasn't sure what to do with my earlier concerns for healing the sick. I resigned myself to focusing on good deeds of community service to aid the lives of others.

Between my roles as a wife, mother, and community servant, my life was active and full. My life seemed relatively complete until, at the age of thirty-four, I saw and read a Bible for the first time in my life. Then, *suddenly*, nothing was the same again. Ever.

'Thy Words Were Found, and I Did Eat Them'

I received the baptism of the Holy Spirit after reading a book called *The Holy Spirit and You*, written by Episcopalian teachers Rita and Dennis Bennett. Nick had taken the kids out for a ride, so I sat down and finished reading this little book. I realized that there was more to be had of God, and I asked Him, as the book had instructed, to baptize me in the Holy Spirit. And instantly I was filled with His presence, having never been in a charismatic meeting, having never heard tongues before.

Suddenly, as I was trying to bring forth a language unknown to me, as I was beginning to speak, I saw words upon the wall of the living room. The words that I was trying to pronounce were moving from the right-hand corner of the wall to the left like a ticker tape.

Later when friends heard that this had happened to me they invited me to a Bible study. It was then that I saw a Bible for the very first time.

When I began to read the Bible, life took on an entirely new dimension. Finally, I knew God's thoughts—they were all written down in black and white, and sometimes red! I could read His words and discover His will, as well as learn His ways through the many descriptions of His acts in the lives of men and women in the Bible.

With a voracious hunger for God's words, I devoured the Scriptures. As the prophet Jeremiah exclaimed, so it was with me: *"Thy words were found, and I did eat them; and thy word was unto me the joy and rejoicing of mine heart: for I am called by thy name, O Lord God of hosts"* (Jeremiah 15:16).

The more I read about God the Father and my Lord Jesus, the more real they became to me. I was so thankful that the Father had sent me the Holy Spirit to be my own personal Teacher and Friend. Daily as I read the Scriptures, the Holy Spirit would open up, reveal, and explain portions of the Word of God to me. I would take a pen and paper with me as I studied and prayed because

I wanted to write down every wonderful thing my Teacher, the Holy Spirit, would speak to my heart. (That is a practice I continue until this day.) The more the Holy Spirit revealed, the more I wanted to commune with Him in prayer. I not only set aside specific time for prayer, I also invited the Holy One to walk with me through every aspect of my life as my Teacher, Counselor, and Friend.

I would also talk with Him about my day. I would simply acknowledge the fact that He, the Holy Spirit, is with me always, and I spoke with Him just as freely as I would with a friend. It was in such times of practicing His presence that I learned to distinguish the voice of the Holy Spirit, both through the Scriptures and within my own spirit.

In 1980, at the age of thirty-seven, I was in prayer when I believe I heard the Holy Spirit say, *I am calling you out of Catholicism.* That was a strange thing to me because I had known no other religion and had been to no other church. All I knew were cathedrals, so that concerned me. But He told me that He would tell me when, and He would tell me how, and not to be concerned. So I left that with Him.

Then one evening while I was doing the dishes the Holy Spirit said, "I want you to go in and tell Nick now that you can no longer worship in Catholicism, and he is going to understand." So I did.

It was as though God arrested Nick for one moment in time as I told him, "Honey, I don't believe I can worship in Catholicism anymore."

He said, "I know."

"Well, I am going to have to leave," I explained.

"I know."

"Okay?"

And Nick said, "Yes."

Then it was as though the moment was over, and Nick asked me if I understood the far-reaching consequences of my decision. I said, "No, I don't."

I do not want to suggest that everyone is to leave the Catholic Church or abandon all Catholic teachings. A big charismatic movement began on Notre Dame's campus in 1968 and spread great revival throughout the world. I only know that God had another plan for me, and I had to be obedient and follow Him to the new church He wanted me to attend.

It Matters Where You Go to Church

The only churches I had ever known were cathedrals with stained glass windows, statues, and candles everywhere. The charismatic churches springing up at that time were basically storefront churches—renovated furniture or paint stores with neon lights. They were so different from what I was used to. But I knew I had to find my pastor—the pastor God had selected for me. I had not yet read Jeremiah 3:15, which states, *"And I will give you pastors according to mine heart, which shall feed you with knowledge and understanding."* Nevertheless, the belief was strong in my heart that God had specifically chosen a pastor to teach me and feed me spiritually.

I just followed my heart, and the Holy Spirit directed my steps to Victory Fellowship, pastored by Bill and Linda McRay. I quickly learned the tremendous value of having pastors who will cover you in prayer and feed you

the pure Word of God. After sitting under the McRays'
teaching and training for six years, I was licensed into
the ministry with my husband's permission. After serving
a two-year internship, I was ordained by my pastors into
full-time ministry.

At Victory Fellowship, I experienced the Father's
overwhelming compassion to heal the sick. The waves of
compassion I experienced as a six-year-old child had
never left me, but now I found a fuller expression to
release. I learned to minister God's life-giving Word and
healing power to people and watch as His goodness
brought healing into their bodies.

The more time I spent in the Word and with the Holy
Spirit, the more I came to see the power of the covenant we
have with the Father through Jesus Christ. God is perfectly
legal in all His ways. He will always work within His own
prescribed laws to manifest His goodness and His love.

His spiritual laws and principles are continually at
work in the earth. I learned through the Scriptures that
we activate God's laws with our words and establish them
with our decisions. Daily we sow into these principles
with our actions and perpetuate them with our attitudes.

When activated, these laws affect our future outcome. Often these laws are triggered in the midst of unexpected situations—situations that interrupt our daily routine to present an opportunity that could easily be overlooked. But our response to such interruptions affects specific elements of future events—either for ourselves or for someone else—as I learned on the way to the store one day in 1992....

Specific Obedience Affects Future Events

In the early part of that year, I was preparing for an overseas trip. About an hour before I was to be at the airport, I needed to make one more run to Target. As I drove over the hill on the road to the shopping plaza, I heard a horrific explosion. Seconds later, my car was being showered with glass. In front of me down the road, two cars had just collided head on. Although the cars were stopped, the glass was still flying.

We were on a busy street in Nashville, but at that moment, no other cars were around. I brought my car to a complete halt at the bottom of the hill and got out to check on the people in the two cars. The first car was tilted upward, leaning diagonally against a telephone pole. There was no way I could get to the occupants of that car. And it was obvious from the position of their car that all of the people inside were unconscious.

The other vehicle, a small, foreign car, was stopped in the middle of the street. A woman got out of the car, covered in blood and screaming hysterically. Coming toward me, she kept saying, "Is he all right? Is he dead? Is he dead?" At the moment, I didn't know who in the world she could be talking about, so I helped her sit down. Fire was darting out from beneath her car.

When I looked inside, I saw a young man, obviously a teenager, who was well over six feet tall. His knees nearly touched his chin in that tiny sports car. As a result of the collision, he suffered a severe head wound, causing his brain tissue to be exposed. His body was convulsing, with involuntary spasms thrashing him back and forth. Because he was so tightly cramped, only his upper body was moving, and his head was swinging back and forth, spurting blood everywhere.

I went over to his side of the car but couldn't open the smashed door. By that time, other cars were passing us, giving the car and me plenty of space. While I stood there pulling on the door, I believe I heard the Lord God say, *Get in the car.*

At that point, I just responded automatically. I didn't really think about what I was doing; I just did it. I guess it had to be that way because no normal human being would jump into a crashed car, and I am certainly not the brave heroine type! In fact, when I entered the ministry, I told God, "I'll serve You, but I want You to know I don't want to be a martyr!"

Glass and shards of metal covered everything. There was hardly any room in that two-seater car, but I squeezed into the bucket seat on the driver's side and tried to get as close to the young man as I could. I picked up something that looked like a T-shirt and held it against his head because he was bleeding so profusely.

Immediately, I heard the Holy Spirit say, *Tell his body to be still and command the bleeding to stop.* When I did that, his body became still and the bleeding stopped. Then I heard the Holy Spirit say, *He doesn't know Jesus. Ask him.* At that moment, all the "mommy" in me rose to the surface, and I drew that child in as close to me as I could and said, "Son, you don't know Jesus, do you?" and he groaned, "No, no." That's all he could get out.

And I said, "Would you receive Jesus Christ as your Lord and Savior? Would you do that?"

"Yeah, yeah," he replied in a foggy-sounding voice. Then his head dropped, and he slumped forward.

The next thing I knew, a paramedic was tapping me on the back, saying, "We'll take him now." Ambulances and fire engines had surrounded the scene. When I stepped out of the car, I had blood all over me. The paramedic was really upset because that contact left me potentially at risk.

All of this happened right in front of a little shopping center. The people from the pharmacy there saw me and took me into their store to wash my hands with special kinds of soap, because they were concerned about the possibility of AIDS.

"I can't believe you got in that car!" someone said.

I didn't bother to explain that God told me to get in there. I just said, "Well, I just knew that I was supposed to do it," and I left it at that.

I found it interesting what other people were thinking about at a time like that. All I could think about was that child in the car. I never heard what happened to him, but I know that if he did die, he went straight on through to be with Jesus.

I boarded an airplane a few hours later and flew to the Czech Republic, where I ministered for two weeks in the former Eastern bloc countries. After I returned home to Nashville, I was speaking with the shampoo technicians where I get my hair done. They mentioned seeing me that day as they drove by the site of the accident.

With amazement they said to me, "Why did you get into that car? What were you doing in that car? What happened?" So there in the back of the salon amongst the shampoo technicians, I gave the testimony of Jesus Christ, giving opportunity once again for people to receive Him as their Savior.

What I did not realize at the time, however, were the far-reaching implications of that incident for my own life. I had no idea that I was being presented with an opportunity for obedience that would build my faith when I needed to believe that God would intervene for my own child who would one day be trapped unconscious in a small car that had been smashed and mangled by a near-fatal accident. But my loving, merciful, and sovereign Father God was working every spiritual principle He could ahead of time on Christina's behalf in preparation for the evil day only months away when Satan would make a claim on her life.

Recalling Your Salvation Experience

In this chapter, I shared my salvation experience with you. Remember the account of the woman who came to our garden to tell me the story about the dogwood tree? I mention this to you because you must also have a salvation experience if you're going to obtain God's best for you in the midst of your situation.

Do you remember the time, the place, or perhaps the people who were involved when you invited Jesus into your life? Journalize the experience on the following lines and try to remember what you were feeling at the time. If you really don't remember ever asking Jesus to be your Savior but you want Him to be, please take the time to turn right now to the prayer of salvation located at the end of this book.

Journal

Journal

_____

_____

_____

_____

_____

_____

_____

_____

_____

_____

_____

_____

_____

_____

_____

_____

3

Awakened by a Friend

*"He giveth power to the faint; and to them that
have no might he increaseth strength."*

ISAIAH 40:29

On May 19, 1992, my day began quietly. At 4:00 in
the morning, the presence of the Holy Spirit came
gently to wake me up, which was not unusual.
Sometimes I would sense His nearness in the middle of
the night, stirring my heart to pray or simply to wake up
and be with Him. At times, I knew I could lie in bed and
pray quietly without disturbing my husband, Nick, as he
slept beside me. Then, at other times, I would know that I

needed to slip out of bed in order to pray and fellowship with God.

So familiar was the voice of my Friend, the Holy One, the precious Holy Spirit, that when I heard Him say to me that morning, *Mary Frances, come downstairs with Me. I want to talk with you about your children,* I had no reason to think that there was anything to be concerned about. As far as I knew, everything was fine with both of our children. But if the Holy One wanted to talk to me about my children, I was delighted to do so. He is, after all, my dearest Friend.

Graces and Mercies

I slipped on my robe, took a pencil and paper, and went down to the living room. The first words the Holy Spirit spoke to my heart that morning puzzled me a little: *Mary Frances, ask God the Father for His graces and mercies for your children.*

Graces and mercies?

I was accustomed to hearing "mercies," for I knew His *mercies* were new every morning. (Lamentations 3:23.) But the word "graces" sounded different to my ear. It didn't upset or alarm me, however. I just responded, "Abba, Father, I ask You to grant Your graces and mercies toward my children today."

Then the Holy Spirit asked me, *Now, you forgive your children for anything they've ever done, right?*

I said, "Oh, yes, Sir." Then I started to wonder, *What are my children doing?* I didn't think Christina and Nicholas were impeccable, but I also knew they weren't dealing drugs on the street corner either.

Nick and I have been blessed with two beautiful and intelligent children. I can say that without a trace of pride because both children were adopted, so they didn't get their good looks or brains from us! Both are successful in their chosen careers. Christina was a production assistant for television, and Nicholas is a chef. Both have a wonderful but very different sense of humor. Nicholas, the youngest, has a very dry, very bright, deadpan sort of wit that never ceases to make me smile. Christina is extremely funny, with a comedic timing that often has us in stitches.

As I thought about the children that morning, I sensed they were okay. As I recalled some of their past antics, I, like any mom, wondered about a few things I was not sure if they had done but I suspected. Yet, regardless of it all, my heart toward them was forgiving. So I said, "Father, I forgive my children of anything and everything they have ever done. Furthermore, Father, I ask You to forgive them, too, please, if they have offended You."

Fellowship: The Vital Element

Such was the essence of that single-minded moment with the Holy Spirit. I continued to spend time with Him in fellowship and praise, just talking with Him, telling Him how much I loved Him, telling Him how dear it was to my heart that He would awaken me to talk about the children. Later, I went back to bed for a few more hours of sleep. My time with Him that morning seemed no different than any other time. Nothing spectacular marked the moment, yet within hours I would discover how profound His questions were to me and how vital my answers were to Him.

When the Holy Spirit awakened me to discuss the children, I had no idea that Satan was about to make a claim for Christina's life. Although she was born again and had a covenant with God, her lifestyle (unknown to me) had opened a door for the enemy to come in and attack her. But our loving, merciful, and sovereign God said, *Not so!* He came around another way to preserve her life and, I believe, to preserve me as well. The Holy One knew I would be deeply grieved if the devil had come in and stolen my daughter's life!

I believe that sometimes the Father extends Himself on my behalf just because of His love for me. In this case, it wasn't so much that I had placed such a great demand upon His Word or was so faithful at putting Him in remembrance of His promises, although that has its place. Instead, it seemed that God prepared the way for my daughter's deliverance primarily because of His love for her and because of the love relationship between Him and me.

When We Know Not How To Pray...

Our fellowship with God is so crucial to experiencing the full beauty and benefit of our covenant relationship with Him. Sometimes we become so preoccupied with an emphasis upon "working the Word" that we forget our relationship with the Author of the Word. God created us to be in fellowship with Him.

Prayer is an aspect of that fellowship. The Father loves us and wants to bless us so much that He sent the Holy Spirit to help us pray. He helps us not only to communicate effectively with the Father in prayer, but also to communicate the will of the Father on the earth through prayer.

I am so grateful for the help of the Holy Spirit in prayer. Romans 8:26,27 AMP tells us that when we are faced with situations and circumstances for which we do not even know what to pray, the Spirit Himself takes hold together with us:

So too the [Holy] Spirit comes to our aid and bears us up in our weakness; for we do not know what prayer to offer nor how to offer it worthily as we ought, but the Spirit Himself goes to meet our supplication and pleads in our behalf with unspeakable yearnings and groanings too deep for utterance.

And He Who searches the hearts of men knows what is in the mind of the [Holy] Spirit [what His intent is], because the Spirit intercedes and pleads [before God] in behalf of the saints according to and in harmony with God's will.

Jesus sent the Holy Spirit to us to be our Helper, our Strengthener, our Comforter. We do not know the future, nor do we have insight into what may lie ahead. But Jesus said that when the Holy Spirit was given, He would lead and guide us into all truth and show us things to come. The Holy Spirit not only tells us about coming situations, He also leads us to pray out the will of God for our future. He does this in advance so His will can already be firmly established whenever we face a particular time of test or trial. Such times come to all of us simply because the enemy of our souls is real, and his goal is to steal, kill, and destroy the blessings of God in our lives. (John 10:10.)

No one is exempt from problems or from facing an evil day. But because of the Holy Spirit Whom God has sent, we can be equipped to master the problems that present themselves. If we will yield to the Holy Spirit and pray or say the words He gives us to pray or say, we can walk successfully through any evil day. And in those moments when we know not what lies ahead, nor how to pray effectively, He—the Holy Spirit of Truth—will give us words to speak, which will bring God's will to pass in our lives or in the lives of those for whom we pray.

The words the Holy Spirit gives us to speak are always in harmony with the will of God because the Holy Spirit *is* God, and His words are formed in the very heart of God the Father. It is therefore so vital to yield to the Holy Spirit's guidance. Whatever we hear Him say—whether it is through the Word of God or by His witness within our spirits—we can speak it with confidence, knowing that it will surely come to pass.

The Holy Spirit's words to us will be the key to turning our situation around, but we must speak to release our God-given authority on the earth.

Death and Life Are in the Power of the Tongue

Words carry a powerful weight in God's economy. He created the heavens and the earth and all that is within them through words. And He continues to uphold all things through the word of His power. When the Father God created man in His image, He gave us the ability to speak words that create and sustain.

Proverbs 18:21 AMP states, *"Death and life are in the power of the tongue, and they who indulge in it shall eat the fruit of it [for death or life]."* The Holy Spirit is with believers to teach, to counsel, and to guide us in releasing the creative force of life through our words. And He has made it so easy for us. All we have to do is speak what He tells us and then believe what He said.

This is how the Spirit of God worked with and through Jesus on the earth. And this is the same way He desires you and me to cooperate with Him today. Jesus said the words He spoke were not His own, but that which were given to Him by God. (John 14:24.) And we know that all Jesus said came to pass because He *only* spoke as the Holy One inspired Him to speak. This is why Jesus spent many nights in prayer. He needed to maintain a vital union with the Holy Spirit in order to fulfill the will of God—and so do we.

I think Jesus' fellowship and communion in prayer with the Holy Spirit had to be the most notable quality about His life. The disciples didn't ask Jesus to teach them how to perform miracles; rather, they said to him, *"Lord, teach us to pray"* (Luke 11:1).

It Matters What YOU Say

As we acknowledge, pay attention to, and follow the leading of the Spirit, He tells us not only what to pray to the Father about a situation, but also what to say in and about a situation. For example, as soon as I learned about Christina's accident, the Holy Spirit immediately spoke to my heart words that told me what to believe and what to speak in the situation. He told me the end of the matter at the beginning.

I've found that when the Holy Spirit speaks to me in such a strong way about a situation in the beginning, there is a purpose. He does so to hold me steady and buffer me against voices or circumstances that will speak contrary to what He has said. The Holy Spirit will also speak truth to us about a situation to help us keep our words in agreement with Him so He can bring His will to pass. You see, although many voices may speak over and about situations in our lives, it matters what *we* say. Our own voice is the deciding voice in our lives. Our own words will determine the course and direction of our days.

Again, Jesus gave us an example of the power of our words in a situation when He spoke and a fig tree withered away to its roots. When the disciples marveled at what His words had accomplished, Jesus replied, saying,

Have faith in God. For verily I say unto you, That whosoever shall say unto this mountain, Be thou removed, and be thou cast into the sea; and shall not doubt in his heart, but shall believe that those things which he saith shall come to pass; he shall have whatsoever he saith.

*Therefore I say unto you, What things soever ye desire, when
ye pray, believe that ye receive them, and ye shall have them.*

MARK 11:22-24

When we trust and have a confident expectation *before*
we see the answer, that is true faith. It is not a hard thing
to believe when we know and are confident in the One
who speaks His very own faith into our hearts. But then
we must give voice or expression to that belief in order to
bring it to pass.

When you say how much you struggle to have faith,
you are simply admitting the poor quality of your
fellowship with God. When you know and love a person
on an intimate level, you know that person's character.
You know how he will act and if his word can be trusted.
If, however, you know a person on only a casual or
superficial level, you are not always sure what he may do
or what you can expect. So it is with our relationship
with God. God is faithful. He is not a man that He
should lie or even need to change His mind. All that He
is and all that He says can be trusted. But you won't be
fully convinced of that if you don't spend enough time
with Him to learn His ways. Although it's possible to

know many facts and details about a person, some things can only be understood by spending time with him. So it is with God the Holy Spirit.

The Holy Spirit has taught me and walked with me through so many trying situations. Perhaps that is why I was so settled when He spoke "life and wholeness for Christina"; I had already experienced His nearness to me in so many situations in life. However, nothing could compare with the journey He and I would embark on that fateful day in May.

You Are a Child of God

Because you are a son or a daughter of God, you are alive unto the voice of God. Please, always remember that God will speak to your heart—your spirit—and not to your head when He wants to communicate with you. What He says to your heart will affect the way you think, react, and respond to relationships, circumstances, and situations in your life. God's voice to you will always reflect the character of His written Word. He waits for the time when you will listen and respond to Him. Can you think of specific occasions to reflect when you have clearly heard God's voice? What Scriptures did He speak to you through? How did you feel after receiving His Word?

Journal

Journal

4

The Accident

"The thief cometh not, but for to steal, and to kill,
and to destroy: I am come that they might have life,
and that they might have it more abundantly."

JOHN 10:10

At the age of nine, Christina was born again and
baptized in the Holy Spirit. Throughout her life, I
had taught her and prayed for my entire family according
to the covenant principles and rights that our heavenly
Father has provided through the blood of His Son.

What I wasn't aware of, however, was that at the time of the accident, Christina's lifestyle choices had legally given the devil an opening to lay claim to her life.

It's a shame that sometimes parents are the last to know about certain things in the lives of our children. When He spoke to me about forgiving the children, I had no idea what was really going on in Christina's life at the time. I'm so grateful for the Holy Spirit's guidance in prayer.

Some have asked me how the accident could occur if God had specifically instructed me to pray for graces and mercies. I do not believe that God failed to do what He was supposed to do. In fact, He did exactly what His laws permitted Him to do.

People forget that there are spiritual laws in operation, just as there are natural, physical laws. Christina was opposing certain spiritual laws established on her behalf. However, there were other spiritual laws that God could exercise legally to step around Satan's onslaught and make a way of escape for Christina. By prompting me to ask Him for graces and mercies for my children, God was enabled—according to His own covenant with me through the blood of Jesus—to raise up a standard of life and wholeness against the spirit of death's attempt to destroy Christina's life.

All this I realized after the fact. But as I stood with my family in the emergency room that day amidst all the emotions of receiving one alarming report after another, all I knew was that the Holy Spirit had promised me life and wholeness for Christina. I clung tightly to those words as I looked upon my daughter's shocking physical appearance and listened to various ones give me the details of Christina's accident that had been pieced together from paramedic and police reports.

The Casualty:
The Enemy Comes in Like a Flood

Christina has worked in television production since she was in college. The morning of her accident, she was on her way to the studio to work on a Statler Brothers television special. As was her custom, she was running late.

She pulled up to the light to turn off West End Avenue and Harding Road in Nashville onto Interstate 440. The light facing her was flashing yellow, so she assumed it was flashing red to the traffic on the street perpendicular to the one she was on, since the cars had come to a full stop. When it was Christina's time to move, she didn't come to a full stop. She made the decision to go through the light. But a milk truck did not have a red light. His light was also flashing yellow, and he just kept coming. Christina's small Honda did not make it to the interstate ramp. The milk truck smashed her car into the abutment of a bridge that passed over the interstate.

The force of the collision cracked a nearby utility pole, and the impact of the crash caused the debris to rip her right ear and break her collarbone, right arm, and right hip. The rest of the car crashed in on Christina, shattering her pelvis, rupturing her spleen, and breaking her ribs. The aorta to her heart was torn in the process. Due to the severity of the impact, Christina's brain was slammed back and forth inside her skull, causing what doctors described as brain shear. Trapped, bleeding internally, and unconscious, Christina was dying.

But grace and mercy had prepared a way out.

That morning, off-duty paramedics in an ambulance were two cars behind Christina. As soon as the crash occurred, they jumped out to help her. As best they could, they crawled through the splattered glass and shattered metal to give Christina an airway until she could be cut free from the vehicle, which at that point was smashed in around her.

When the utility pole came down, it took out the electricity for the main section of West Nashville. Therefore, all the traffic lights were out, making it very difficult for ambulances, police cars, and fire trucks with emergency equipment to weave their way through traffic to get to the accident scene. We were later told that by the time the other ambulance and fire truck arrived with the "jaws of life"—a tool used to cut the car apart— Christina had died.

According to the report given to us, it took twenty to thirty minutes to cut Christina out of the car. By the time they did, however, she was no longer breathing and her heart had stopped. So they began using the defibrillation paddles to jolt her heart into responding. On the third try, they secured a heartbeat. But when they did, Christina's hands, arms, and legs curled and drew up into near fetal position, exhibiting the full extent of her brain damage.

In a situation where every second mattered, it was as though time had screeched to a halt. We were told that everything came to a total standstill.

All this occurred at the height of morning rush hour. No signals were functioning because the accident had knocked out key power lines. Traffic was in complete mayhem. The traffic jam forced the ambulance to drive on the median and across front yards, making it extremely difficult to arrive at the accident scene quickly. The paramedics called for the Life Flight helicopter to lift Christina from the scene of the accident to the nearest hospital. But once the pilot arrived, there was no place for him to land, so they made the decision to transport her by ambulance to the closest Level I Trauma Center Hospital.

From the time the accident occurred until the time Christina was lifted out and transported to the hospital, nearly one hour had passed. Yet, in the midst of utter chaos, God was ordering the steps of all those who would come to Christina's aid. When the enemy rushed in like a flood with casualty, my merciful Father God had already moved out ahead to lift up a barrier against him.

The Decision: Life and Wholeness in the Shadow of Death

Five hours after the Holy Spirit awakened me to pray, I found out why He wanted to discuss the children. I had gone to the beauty shop that morning, so people were trying to find me to let me know what had happened. Around 9:00 A.M., one of the secretaries at Victory Fellowship Church called to tell me that Christina had been in a terrible automobile accident and taken to the hospital. Nick was already on his way there, and one of Nick's nurses was coming to pick me up.

No sooner had I hung up the phone than I believe I heard the voice of the Holy Spirit speak words that seemed audible to me because they were so distinct and clear: *Mary Frances, life and wholeness for Christina; life and wholeness.*

Immediately, everything became sure. I won't say that I felt "calm" because, after all, I am a mom, and hearing that my daughter was in such serious condition gripped my emotions as intensely as it would any mother. But the Holy Spirit took hold of my spirit, which took hold of the "mom" part of my soul, and by His grace, *truly* all was well with me.

The nurse who came to pick me up and take me to the hospital to join Nick and the family is a Christian. On the way, she said, "Well, we need to pray. Let's pray for Christina."

I replied, "Yes, we do need to pray. Let's pray for everybody else."

The subtle significance of my own words surprised even me. From the depths of my heart, I was sure of Christina's outcome. But my heart went out to my husband, my son, and the rest of the family. Both sides of our family live in Nashville. I knew that, with the grandparents, aunts, uncles, and cousins gathered together, it was going to be an emotionally charged situation. Important decisions were going to have to be made. I knew that. Everybody needed to feel secure. So during that fifteen-

minute ride to the hospital, we prayed for peace and
great wisdom for everyone.

When we arrived at the emergency room, family and
friends had already gathered. I was the last one to arrive.
The family had already been told the severity of
Christina's condition, and they were having a very
difficult time. Some families are closer than others. Our
family is extremely close.

My husband's side of the family is Italian, and my
side is German-Irish. Thus, there tends to be a lot of
volatility when emotions are expressed. Our children are
the only grandchildren on Nick's side, so his family had
given Christina much of their attention and were very
distressed by her accident.

Besides all that, Christina was the "star-spangled
girl" to them. She was everything you'd ever want your
daughter to be: beautiful, talented, intelligent, a student
government leader, and an outstanding athlete. Christina
was an overly accomplished child whom everyone was
proud of. Knowing that she was in a fight for her life
was shocking and extremely difficult for the family to
handle emotionally.

In addition to family and friends flooding the emergency room, the media was present. The Varallo family opened their first restaurant more than eighty years ago in Nashville, and so they have an established name in the food industry throughout the Southeast. Once news of our daughter's accident became known, both radio and television reporters showed up. Christina's accident was not just a tragedy for our family; it also became a human-interest story for the local media.

By the time I arrived at the emergency room, Christina was in surgery, and emotions were already running high as family and friends gathered. Normally, you would wait on a particular floor reserved for the family of those undergoing surgery. But because so many people were showing up at the hospital to be with us, it wasn't long before the hospital graciously provided us with a conference room where we could all gather. The halls were jam-packed with people. In fact, it seemed as though people were everywhere—either commenting on the accident or trying to find out what had happened.

Nick had arrived at the hospital only minutes before me. When I found him in the crowd, we held each other briefly. Then before I really had a chance to say anything about what I believed the Lord had spoken to me concerning the situation, Nick and I listened as an attending physician gave us the litany of Christina's injuries. Both of us were crying as we heard the severity and extent of her injuries. Who could ever imagine that one's child would experience such a horrendous trauma?

As we stood there crying, I turned to Nick and said, "Life and wholeness for Christina; the Lord spoke that to my heart."

Nick fastened his eyes on me and just said, "Okay, Honey." My husband is a very wise man, brilliant in so many ways. I could see the wheels in his mind turning as he tried to gather his composure while at the same time listen to me and take account of what I was saying.

"Mary Fran, do you understand the seriousness of Christina's injuries?" he asked me.

"Perhaps not medically as you do, but I do know that this is serious," I replied.

"They are trying to save her life."

As doctors explained the facts of Christina's injuries and condition, a deluge of devastating reports engulfed us. One negative prognosis followed another. The doctors had performed major abdominal surgery because of the ruptured spleen. Afterward, it was discovered that her chest cavity began to swell. An arteriogram revealed that Christina's aorta was torn.

This injury alone, they informed us, was serious enough to have killed her. But Christina continued to live. The doctors admitted they were surprised she survived the abdominal surgery, so their expectations were low that she would live through an additional surgery, particularly since it was open heart surgery, requiring them to cut off her blood flow from the waist down. The attending surgeon gave us a very realistic picture of her chance of survival because it seemed just too much to ask that she could live through such a procedure in her already critically injured condition. Doctors expressed their concern that even if Christina did live, she could be a paraplegic.

We waited for hours for the surgeons to come out and meet with us after the operation. I will never forget the heart surgeon who came into the conference room where everybody was waiting. It seemed as though half of Nashville was waiting there with us. The surgeon had the biggest grin on his face when he said, "The surgery was textbook perfect! She's doing fine." Then he qualified his statement: "What I mean by fine is that she has survived the surgery. We were able to quickly get in and out of the procedure that cut off the blood supply. There is no paralysis at all from the surgery. It's just remarkable!"

There was no time to celebrate that victory because immediately another team of surgeons wanted to meet with us. This time, several neurosurgeons sat down with us to explain that the damage to Christina's brain had been so severe that there was nothing they could do. All X-rays showed that her brain was continuing to fill with blood and air. They had no idea where the air was coming from, but the damage was so massive that they had resolved to do nothing. Again, we were given a bleak forecast: "Your daughter may not live through the night."

Stagger Not at the Promise When Faced With the Problem

It was 11:00 P.M. Christina had been through several hours of surgery off and on since 8:30 that morning. Her doctors warned us before they began each procedure, "This could be it." But Christina continued to live. Finally, we were allowed to be with her.

Nick and I held each other and our son, Nicholas, as the three of us walked quietly into the surgical intensive care unit. Our steps paced to the rhythmic ticking of the life support machines measuring Christina's pulse and breath. Slowly, we turned the corner only to come to an abrupt, simultaneous halt at the sight of her. It was as though all of us gasped and lost our breath at once. Our eyes burned with a sudden rush of tears that would not stop. No description could have prepared us for the shock of what we saw. The three of us tightened our grip on each other as we looked at Christina for the first time since her accident.

Christina was on full life support. Respirators, wires, pumps, and hoses were inserted and connected to her on every side. She wasn't able to sustain any bodily function on her own. Her body was extremely swollen. Plastic splints were fastened to her legs in an attempt to keep them straight, but doctors hadn't been able to do anything with her right arm because of the swelling. They simply wrapped it in a splint to prevent the broken bones from protruding through the skin.

A surgeon later explained that none of Christina's broken bones were set—and her hip, pelvis, ribs, right arm, and collar bone were all fractured. Apparently, throughout the course of the traumatic surgeries she endured, everything else was so vital that setting fractured bones was low on the priority list. Broken bones were a mild thing in contrast to our daughter's torn and hemorrhaging internal organs. Besides, none of the doctors expected Christina to survive at that point; thus, her bones were never set.

As the three of us looked at Christina lying there completely comatose, we just held on to each other and cried. Our beautiful Christina did not look anything like herself at all. The front of her head was shaven, and a brain monitor was inserted into her skull to measure pressure produced by the blood that continued to cause her brain to swell. On the right side of her head, the hair was still matted with blood.

I made my way through all the equipment surrounding Christina and came as close as I could to her bedside. I remembered hearing from others who had been comatose that a person in that condition may still be aware. My first thought was to comfort Christina and let her know what was happening. Bending down to kiss her cheek, I whispered in her left ear, "Christina, you've been in a terrible accident. But listen and understand me. You need to know that God said, 'Life and wholeness' for you, Christina. You'll live and not die. Wholeness belongs to you. So regardless of what you hear, I want you to know life and wholeness is what God said."

After speaking those words to my daughter, I reached over to touch her matted hair and saw that her ear was moving. I called the surgeon over and said, "There's something wrong here." Sure enough, the doctor pulled her hair back to discover that Christina's ear had been practically torn off! Immediately, he called for the maxillofacial surgeon to come in, clean her up, and sew her ear back on.

When the doctor injected Christina to anesthetize the area, he said that she pulled away from the needle. He found the response surprising yet explained it away, saying, "The body can still respond to pain despite brain damage."

"Well, then," I said, thinking of all the bones they had said were broken but had not yet been set, "would you all please remember that as you're turning her body every which way!"

Despite the lateness of the hour, friends continued to come to the hospital to be with us. My pastors, Bill and Linda McRay of Victory Fellowship, had been one of the first to come be with our family, and they remained with us throughout the evening. Their presence was such a comfort. Everything Pastor Bill had ever taught me about faith in God's Word was now being put to the test. Without that teaching, I know I would not have made it through this ordeal. The Word I had been taught laid a solid foundation that held me steady, so when the Spirit spoke to my heart, I had the capacity to embrace His words as absolute truth. It had been twelve years up to that point that Pastor Bill had taught me the integrity of God's Word. Now, in the midst of crisis, he and Linda came to stand with Nick and me to help assure that our faith did not falter.

As soon as they arrived that afternoon, Pastor Bill walked straight to me and asked me point blank, "What are you believing, Mary Frances?" I knew exactly what he meant. I told him what I believed God told me, and then I said, "I know it looks crazy and maybe I sound crazy to everybody else, but I know that God said life and wholeness for Christina. And I believe that's just the way it is and that's the way it's going to be."

He stood there very quietly, listening intently with his eyes searching mine. Finally, he said, "I do believe you. Well, all right. I got you." And that was it. A year later, Pastor Bill explained to me that from that point on, he and Linda "scotched" me, that is to say they supported and helped hold me steady in my stance of faith. As a former Air Force mechanic, Pastor Bill explained their role in prayer for me as functioning like the logs wedged securely in front of a jet's tires after it lands to "scotch" it in place to prevent it from rolling or moving its position.

The situation looked so grim. The neurosurgeon said there was only a twenty-percent chance of Christina coming out of the coma—and if she did, she would not know what planet she was on, and that was a generous assessment. From all appearances, the situation did look bleak.

But there I was, going for the whole ball of wax! I had heard God say, "Life and wholeness," and I believed Him, even when life was the last thing on anybody else's agenda for Christina.

I already knew that I would have to contend against what I could see regarding Christina's condition until God's words about her came to pass. And I never questioned that they would.

Each time we looked at Christina, lying limp and essentially lifeless, her condition shouted the very opposite of what the Holy Spirit had promised me. But I believed Him. He had already proven His love and truthfulness to me in so many ways. Trusting Him was not the difficulty. The difficulty was looking at the horrible attack against my daughter's life. The reality of the trauma was indeed staggering. But I held tightly to His promise and allowed the Holy One's own words to uphold me by their power. And in that place of leaning wholly on Him, He enabled me to stand and stagger not.

With every new physical report, the prognosis was increasingly dismal and grim. In the valley of that experience, we weren't confronted by merely one mountain.

It seemed as though we faced an entire mountain range! Doctors offered no hope. All but one were reluctant to suggest even a possibility of Christina's improving. Death had cast its long, foreboding shadow. But in the valley of the shadow of death, while a multitude of voices echoed disaster, the words of the Holy One settled the matter for me.

Mary Frances, life and wholeness for Christina, He said.

And I believed Him.

Knowing the Holy Spirit

I believe it is in your heart to know the Holy Spirit as you've never known Him before. In this book, I have tried to share with you how you can know Him better. Please remember that the Holy Spirit is always trying to help you become better acquainted with Him, with our Father God, and with our Lord Jesus.

Suppose you were to say, "Holy Spirit, I really want to know You better. How do I do that?" He might respond to you as He did to me when He said, *Mary Frances, you will have to practice My presence.*

I will never forget the moment I stood with a big wicker clothes basket loaded with the children's dirty clothes, making my way with the children to wash the laundry down in the "dungeon" (as I called it)—the old, stone basement in our home.

"So, Holy One," I said, "I'm getting ready to do the wash. Would You like to do the wash with the children and me?"

It was just amazing to me that God didn't mind washing clothes with me in the basement with my children running and playing and yelling all around me. But that's what I was doing, and He was glad for my fellowship. I was a young wife and mom doing "young wife and mom" things.

My point is this: What are you doing right now? Whatever you are doing, that's where the Lord will meet you—in the reality of your *now*. Take a moment to invite Him into the experience of all you do. That is the way you will come to know Him in a greater way. And the better you know Him, the more you will trust Him. The more complete your knowledge of Him, the more absolute your trust of Him will be.

Times of need or crisis come to all of us. But when you know Him, you will hear Him. And when you hear His voice, you will be comforted by His words and strengthened by the magnificence of His presence as He leads you to your miracle.

Journal

Journal

5

Fear Not, Only Believe

"Fear thou not; for I am with thee: be not dismayed; for I am thy God: I will strengthen thee; yea, I will help thee; yea, I will uphold thee with the right hand of my righteousness."

ISAIAH 41:10

"Your daughter is severely brain damaged, Mrs. Varallo," the surgeon said grimly. "If there is *any* chance at all of getting a response from her, it will most likely be a response to her parent's voice. Could you go home and make a tape for her?"

"It just so happens that I already have."

99

A few months prior, I'd had such a strong urge to record a tape of only healing Scriptures. At first, I thought it was just a dumb idea. *Who needs to put out another recording of healing Scriptures when so many others have already done that?* I thought. But I couldn't shake the desire. After a while, I realized that the Holy Spirit was prompting me to do it, so I finally obeyed and recorded the tape.

Now the surgeon was asking me for a recording of my voice with the hope of prompting a response from Christina. I was stunned when I realized the thoroughness of the Holy Spirit's preparation for divine intervention on behalf of our family.

My secretary dashed out and brought back a cassette player with headphones and a copy of my healing Scripture tape to play for Christina. Gently I slipped the headphone over Christina's good ear. From that moment, there was hardly a time when her spirit wasn't being saturated with the Word of God concerning healing. While life-giving oxygen, intravenous tubes, and other machines helped support Christina's physical body, God's medicine supplied divine virtue to strengthen and sustain her spirit and effect a miracle and healing in her body as well. When others suggested bringing in tapes of music from her workplace, Nick would always respond in a matter-of-fact way, "We have a tape. It's a tape of her mother reading healing Scriptures. That's the tape we will play." Eventually, there were other tapes.

It was around 2:00 A.M. before everything began to settle down. Christina had endured two major surgeries and untold tests, yet continued to live. We had met with a number of surgeons and assorted specialists. The hospital personnel graciously let us sleep in the conference room. We were exhausted and emotionally drained from the day's disturbing events. So much had happened. Each of us was preoccupied as we sorted through our own thoughts and feelings, trying to make sense of this senseless tragedy.

What is going on inside Christina in the midst of all this? Is she even vaguely aware of what's happening? Countless questions collided inside my mind, but I was just too tired to ponder the answers. I felt numb, yet strangely peaceful. It almost scared me to see how easy it was to go to sleep, but sleep we did.

Morning came quickly. And with it came the realization that the nightmarish images in my head were real. A horrible accident had indeed happened. Our beautiful daughter was indeed comatose, connected to full life support, and not expected to live through the night. We were indeed embroiled in the battle of our lives. But suddenly, quietly, words drifted to the surface of my thoughts and stilled my mind: *Life and wholeness for Christina....* "Yes," I sighed, speaking quietly. "You promised it, Holy One, and I believe You."

Going to the Other Side

It was the morning after, and we prepared ourselves to face the day. Only God knew what it might bring. At 6:30 A.M. a woman from our church named Agnes Stewart came to see us.

As we stood talking by the surgical information desk, I looked up to see Agnes walking full speed ahead, straight toward us. Agnes, a tall woman of impressive stature, is quiet, reserved, and very "together." I could tell by her pace that she had something specific to say. I also knew that Agnes would never say nor do anything unless God directed her, so I was very excited to hear what she might have to say.

After I introduced her to Nick, Agnes went straight to the point of her visit. "I know that you're busy, and I won't keep you from what you have to do. But, Nick," she asked, "do you know the story about the time Jesus told the disciples to get in the boat and go to the other side of the Sea of Galilee? Do you remember that, in the midst of their trip across the sea, a terrible storm arose?"

"Yes," he replied.

"Well," she continued, very matter-of-factly and without emotion, "you need to know that the Spirit of the Lord spoke to my heart in prayer. And just as those disciples made it to the other side despite the storm simply because *Jesus said* they were going to the other side, that's the way it is for Christina as well. Nick, you're going to the other side."

Then she looked at me and asked, "Do you understand that?" I nodded, absolutely dumbfounded by the ways of God to send this marvelous woman to speak so boldly to our hearts. As she turned to leave, Agnes looked back and said, "Now remember: You're going to the other side. God said it, and that's what will happen."

That phrase immediately became our anthem. When people called or came by to ask how it was going, we'd reply, "God said life and wholeness for Christina, and we're going to the other side!"

Through the Storm

It wasn't natural to feel as steady as I did. I can only attribute it to the strength of God's mighty hand holding me. I cannot truthfully say I felt calm. On the contrary, my thoughts and emotions were nearly frantic! But a deep, abiding peace buoyed me up above the turbulent waves of emotion crashing against my mind.

When Jesus spoke the words "go to the other side" to His disciples, immediately Satan stirred up a storm so violent, it terrified even the most seasoned fishermen among them. Whipped and tossed by vicious winds and ravaging waves, the disciples forgot the Master's words. They also forgot how to use their faith. What they saw and felt, they believed they could not control. Therefore, they fearfully surrendered to the situation that threatened to consume them.

The enemy's tactics of intimidation have not changed. If he can distract us with what we see and feel and persuade us by force of fear to believe we are powerless before his onslaught, our response will be no different than the disciples. They cried, "Lord, don't You even care that we are perishing? Hey, can't You see we're drowning over here? Aren't You going to do something?"

Jesus awoke, arose, and rebuked the winds. But then He turned to the disciples and said, "Where was your faith?"—in other words, "What's the matter with you? You could have spoken to the winds just like I did!"

Faith is released through our words. That is why we must have confidence in the words we speak. And in order to have confidence in our words, we must have confidence in the words God speaks. But we cannot have confidence in the words God speaks if we have not gained confidence in *the Spirit of God*, Who speaks those words into our spirit. It all comes back to knowing God intimately and trusting Him completely. It all comes back to our relationship with Him.

I wasn't basing what I believed solely upon a mere impression of what I believed I had heard Him say. I trusted what He had spoken to my heart because I was secure in my relationship with my heavenly Father. I was secure in the knowledge of His character as revealed in the Word.

I can't express or even explain my faith in Him apart from the context of relationship. My confidence in the Father's words to me came from a life of talking with Him and listening to Him. It came from a life of prayer since I was a little child.

Even when we do not know all the right words to say or we do not comprehend the finer points of doctrine, our love for Him will release to us the reality of the integrity and honor He maintains toward His own Word. And our relationship with Him will persuade and convince us of His faithfulness and establish our hearts in the truth of His promises.

Impressions we receive or think we receive are not enough. Impressions can come from both sides of the spirit realm—God or the enemy. Impressions can come from your own soul, based on your own thoughts, desires, or inclinations. But in the midst of a crisis, you must be able to discern the difference between your soul and your spirit, for God will speak directly to your spirit by His Spirit.

We must examine ourselves and ask, *Where did that impression come from?* Most of us don't really understand the deceptive angel of light; we're often too busy trying to disengage our own souls—our intellect, our will, and our emotions.

Only the written Word of God, the two-edged sword of the Spirit, can divide between the soul and the spirit and discern the thoughts and intents of our hearts. For this reason, it is vital that we present ourselves before God daily to fellowship with Him through His Word.

God's words are His thoughts, His desires. God's words pulsate with His passion and emotion. When we receive His words into our spirit, our thoughts begin to take shape in agreement with His thoughts. Our ways begin to resemble His ways.

So, you see, knowing God and knowing His Word are inseparable. We cannot truly know God apart from His Word.

'Time Is Mine'

One afternoon, I pulled away from everyone just to be alone with the Holy Spirit, Whom Jesus described as our Helper, our Strengthener, our Standby. All the Holy Spirit was sent to be for us was what I needed Him to be for me at that moment.

Walking down the hallway with my journal in hand, I focused on breathing in and breathing out, intentionally and aggressively resisting the pressure that sought to suffocate me. I slipped into a crowded elevator, pressed a number, and then stepped out onto whatever floor we reached next. I walked until I found a vacant cove around the corner from a waiting room. Soaking up the silence, I

stood and looked out the bay window, enjoying the sun.
At that moment, I heard the Holy Spirit quietly say, *I am
containing her. All is not as it seems to you.* I wrote those
words in the journal I had with me, grateful that I had
picked it up before I took this little walk.

I stood alone in the hospital hallway that day,
pondering the Holy Spirit's words to me. When I sensed
Him say He was "containing" Christina, I understood
that to mean she would be as He declared her to be—that
she would be as I *said*, not as she appeared to me. He
wasn't saying that He was containing her in her sickness,
but that she was contained whole in Him. He caused me
to know that I just had to keep saying what I'd been
saying until what I saw in this realm lined up with what
God had spoken about her from His realm.

How can I pray her through this, Lord? I thought. *How
do I draw Your eternal will—healing, life, and wholeness—
through the gateway of time? How do I extend my faith to
pull in a miracle from Your realm into mine? We've been in
this battle for two weeks. That's a long time!* (I had no idea
what a long time it was going to be!) Right then I heard
Him speak so distinctly: *Time belongs to Me, Mary Frances.*

She is not as she appears to you. Leave it alone. Time belongs to Me.

The peace released by the presence of the Holy Spirit and the words He spoke to me became the only anchor for my soul in the midst of our storm. Daily we were buffeted by facts that were just as real, unrelenting, and fearsome as the winds and waves that assailed the disciples. But just as often, I repeated what God had said to me. It was a means of speaking peace against the unrelenting torrent of reports that challenged God's words of life and wholeness for Christina.

Christina had a lot of problems with her lungs and frequently had some fluid and infection in them. Her heart, weakened by a damaged aorta, would beat as fast and fierce as a runaway freight train. Then her brain pressure would soar exceedingly, leaving doctors baffled about the cause. There was always the possibility of inserting a shunt in an attempt to siphon off the blood that continued to fill her brain. But everyone—our family as well as the doctors—felt uneasy about conducting another surgery. Christina had survived so much, and she continued to do so. But we all knew it would be pushing it to attempt one more thing unless it was absolutely necessary. Between her racing heart and extreme brain pressure, Christina was in a constant state of emergency.

In addition to all this, one day while Christina was still in ICU, we received a call to gather the family and come in. Somehow, Christina had contracted influenza (the worst type), and she had no immune system to combat it.

Crisis after crisis continued to hit our daughter—and us in the process. But each time, for a short time, her heart rate would suddenly slow down, her pressure would subside, and her breathing would stabilize. She continued to survive.

Her condition could change at a moment's notice, so Nick and I were at the hospital constantly during those first two weeks. So were countless friends and family members, who came to talk, to wait, and to pray with us.

Throughout this entire ordeal, Pastor Bill and Linda continued to come to the hospital daily to sit with us for hours. Each time I saw them, I thanked God inwardly for the decisions they made and the price they paid to start Victory Fellowship twelve years prior to that time. But even beyond that, I was grateful for all the decisions that had enabled them to follow the calling on their life.

I praised God for the pastors who pioneered against all odds to raise up churches where the Word of God is taught and the Spirit of God is given access. I am firmly convinced that it will become more and more important for all of us to attend churches that will feed us the uncompromised Word of God. I imagined what our lives might have been like if we had not been trained to stand in faith, to hope against hope, to trust in God for all Jesus died to provide.

As time went on, we decided to have food catered in because there were always so many people at the hospital. I felt as though I needed to take care of everyone and make sure they were all okay.

One day during the second week of Christina's hospitalization, Pastor Bill observed me as I ran around checking on people and making arrangements for food in between talking with doctors. He pointed at me and said sternly, "Come here!"

Looking me full in the face, he said, "If you continue to wear yourself out physically, it will become next to impossible for you to continue to stay in there spiritually for Christina. So you have a decision to make: Do you want her to live, or do you want her to die? You can't continue to run around trying to take care of everyone else and still stay strong in faith on Christina's behalf."

My husband was standing there and heard what Pastor Bill had said. He agreed with the soundness of the pastor's advice. Pastor Bill's words jolted me—a definite reality check. Both Nick and Pastor Bill could tell that I was wearing down, but I had been too busy to notice. So Nick made arrangements for additional care for Christina. By that time, Christina had been moved from intensive care to special care. Although she had special-care nurses, Nick hired additional nurses to come in during the night specifically to watch over and care for her.

Christina looked so bad. God was purposeful in telling me she was *not* as she appeared. When friends came to visit, some fainted and others were taken aback at the sight of her. It was true that her appearance was more than startling. Everything about how she looked— even how her body would sometimes involuntarily jerk— reflected the full extent of the tragedy she had survived.

Nothing about Christina resembled the beautiful girl we all knew—the girl that her family was holding on to.

The medical staff often averted their eyes from us when they checked her vital signs, trying somehow to conceal the utter hopelessness they felt in the face of her impossible condition. I almost felt sorry for their struggle to reconcile the fact that they genuinely had no hope to offer. Fortunately, our hope was holding on to the only One who could help in this desperate time of need.

When I observed the way the nurses handled or spoke about Christina, I realized they didn't visualize her as we did. We treated her as our beloved daughter, sister, friend. They viewed her as a patient who was in a persistent vegetative state. Of course, that was understandable considering her condition. They hadn't known or seen Christina before the accident, so how could they relate to the image of her that was so clear in our minds? But I wanted them to "see" Christina as the person we knew her to be.

Change What You See

I had a picture of Christina when she was horseback riding, looking absolutely magnificent astride a beautiful palomino horse. We had the photograph enlarged to poster size and placed it over Christina's bed in the intensive care unit. Every time a doctor, nurse, or technician worked on Christina, that image of her—vibrant, healthy, and beautiful—is what they saw. I noticed that they began to talk about her in the present tense. For example, they'd ask, "Is horseback riding what she likes to do?" instead of, "Is that what she liked to do?"

The hospital staff, while doing everything within their power to help Christina, did not expect Christina to survive. They did not hide their negative beliefs, which were based simply on the facts of the situation. I couldn't fault them for doing their job. My positive beliefs, however, were based simply on the higher truths of the Word of God. But when I hung the poster of Christina, I noticed a slight change in how the medical staff spoke about her.

Their adjustment in tense and tone toward Christina may have seemed insignificant, but it was the difference between speaking words that would keep her life connected to the present and words that would relegate her life to the past. It was a subtle difference that made all the difference in the world—the difference between having life and wholeness or *not*.

Christina was indeed suspended between life and death. Everything in the natural was overwhelmingly against her. The facts of the situation were undeniable. But I was not attempting to deny the facts. I intended to do my part to change them. And the only way to change what was seen was to connect with the unseen and speak life-filled words according to the higher reality already established in the realm of God.

Each person who worked with Christina had a part to play. The doctors, nurses, and technicians who viewed her image in the poster began to talk about Christina—still in her comatose state—as though she were still the vibrant and alert woman in that photograph. They made reference to her in the present tense, rather than speaking of her in the past.

Whether or not they understood the principle, the medical staff was being schooled along in faith. As each one viewed the healthy image of Christina, they did what Romans 4:17 in *The Amplified Bible* describes as speaking *"of the nonexistent things that [He has foretold and promised] as if they [already] existed."* In this case, God had promised life and wholeness. Now even the hospital personnel were, as the *King James Version* states it, *"calling those things which be not as though they were."*

I didn't get in the face of this person or that person saying, "God said thus and such...," trying to make them believe what I believed. It didn't seem to be important that the doctors or nurses didn't believe Christina would recover. Nor was it particularly vital that they were vocal in their disbelief. Their refusal to believe that she could recover wasn't very encouraging, but it wasn't vital to Christina's recovery. The important thing for me was that *I* continued to believe God and trust in what He said to me. Somehow, it was enough that their words bent just a bit from the past tense to coincide with the desired end.

I sensed the Father's heart toward Christina. She is His daughter as well as mine. He—the Father—wanted life and wholeness for her. His Son had purchased that for her. The significant thing was not so much a matter of me trying to declare something in order to persuade or pull people into alignment with *my* belief and *my* confession concerning Christina. No, the Father Himself was seeking to bring all of us into agreement with *Him* and *His* desires for Christina. And the Father's desire for her was life and wholeness.

That desire was being defied and challenged by circumstances, which loomed larger with every passing day. But despite the horror and initial shock of the accident and its resulting trauma, the greatest difficulty for all of us was still ahead. Each of us was about to learn a lesson in endurance.

Time Belongs to God

In this chapter, I shared with you how I believe I heard God say, *Time belongs to Me, Mary Frances. Leave it alone. Christina is not as she appears to you.*

God does not exist in time—we do. Our whole universe does. We mark events on earth by time, but God is timeless. He is eternal; He has no beginning or end.

I had much to learn about God's timing during that difficult period of my life, and I am still in the process of learning. I had much to learn and am still learning about patience as well. I must confess to you that patience is a quality the Holy Spirit works on a lot with me.

Can you recall times in your life when God was teaching you the gift of patience? Use the lines that follow to reflect on a few of those instances. So please don't mind the times you spend with Him learning patience. He truly does know what is best, and He is only preparing you for times in your life when you will have need of patience.

Journal

6

Against All Odds

"O Lord my God, I cried out to You, and You healed me."

PSALM 30:2 NKJV

Three weeks after the accident, Christina was still in a coma. I had been speaking the words "life and wholeness" over her repeatedly, doing my best to remember that she was not as she appeared.

But it was difficult, very difficult, to ignore the way she appeared.

Christina's eyes remained shut. Her head rolled and drooped lifelessly to one side. Sometimes her jaws would lock in spasms and her teeth would clamp down tightly on her tongue, nearly biting it off as spurts of blood shot forth.

Christina's arms and hands were bent and drawn up so tightly that they resembled chicken wings, a phenomenon known as posturing. Heavy casts held her legs in place in an attempt to prevent her feet from drawing up. (If her feet had been allowed to draw up or inward, the ligaments and tendons in her legs and toes would have soon stretched and pulled in the wrong direction. Then when it was time for her to attempt to walk again, she would have been forced to walk on tiptoes rather than flat-footed.) But despite the heavy casts intended to hold her body in place, Christina's body continued to jerk and thrash about from muscle spasms.

Nurses would move Christina around frequently despite her broken hip and pelvis to help avoid bedsores. They also placed her in a strange-looking wheelchair with sheets wrapped around her because her body was so contorted. They would tie her into the chair with sheets. But because she had no muscle control, when the involuntary spasms would hit, she would start sliding out of the chair. Often I would sit on the floor and support her heavily casted legs and feet to prevent her from becoming tangled in the chair or, worse, crashing to the floor.

We continued to hire special private nurses to provide additional care for her, since the special care staff could not devote exclusive, round-the-clock treatment for her. Although the staff would leave her catheter and solid waste bags exposed, I sought to retain as much dignity for Christina as possible. I asked them to keep the door closed so she wouldn't be so exposed before everyone.

Our private-duty nurses helped keep Christina clean. But in light of the fact that she had a breathing tube in her throat, a feeding tube in her stomach, and bags attached to catch her bodily fluids, it was a struggle to help her look as good as possible. Some of my friends would come in to be with us, but they would be too overwhelmed by what they saw to carry on a decent conversation. Many of Christina's friends came to visit her and to encourage us, but most grew weak at the sight of her. All this helped me realize early on that it is so important to present a faith picture for the souls of people to connect with so they can understand that all is well. Otherwise, they can easily get carried off into despair by what they see.

Although Christina was no longer connected to a respirator, she still required a steady supply of oxygen because she wasn't able to breathe unaided. A tracheotomy was performed to allow a tube to pump moisturized oxygen directly into her lungs through her neck. This opening needed to be cleaned frequently by suction to remove the build-up of fluid. However, Christina developed a reaction to the suctioning. In the midst of the treatment, her bronchial tubes would go into spasm. Whenever that happened, her oxygen tank alarm would go off and we'd know we had only about two minutes to stabilize her oxygen supply. This would usually trigger a rapid heart rate that seemed to spiral out of control.

And so the cycle went, day after day, week after week, until we were well into our second month with no visible change in sight. Christina's condition didn't worsen, but neither was she improving. She looked about as far from any appearance of life and wholeness as a person could be without being dead.

Doctors would tell us, "You know, this is as good as it's going to get with Christina. She will never look any different or be any different than she is right now—that is, *if* she continues to live." Yet Nick and I refused to accept their assessment of her condition as complete. We appreciated the skill they brought to the situation in sustaining Christina through her massive injuries, but their words were not the final decree. The Spirit of God had spoken to my heart before the ordeal ever began. And throughout the course of many weeks, even months, He continued to affirm His involvement in the matter.

For example, there were times when the doctors would come in while making their rounds, and I would say something or ask a question that was prompted by the Spirit of God, revealing facts previously undiscovered about Christina's condition. One such situation involved the extremely high fevers that plagued her repeatedly. Christina's temperature would often spike as high as 105 degrees without explanation. The medical staff would do everything they could do to bring down the fever, such as placing her between cooling blankets. But the only explanation they could offer was to say, "It's brain fever.

This happens with people who have experienced the type of injury Christina has."

One day my reply was simple and direct: "I understand there is such a thing as brain fever, but that's not what this is. How do you account for the high white blood cell count that you have found in Christina?" I hadn't known about that. The doctors knew they had never mentioned that fact to me. But in that moment, the Holy Spirit revealed it to me for a purpose.

The trauma surgeon in charge that day asked, "How did you know about that?" The puzzled look on his face revealed his obvious surprise. I didn't answer him. I simply restated my question.

"My question to you is this: Where is the infection? Clearly there is a site of infection. Otherwise," I said, "the white cell count wouldn't be so elevated. Therefore, this is not just brain fever."

The team of doctors just looked at me and glanced around at one another. To be honest, I was more shocked than they were by that revelation. But apparently, it was a vital disclosure because a team of infectious disease medical specialists were called in. Their findings proved that what I said was true. But no one could find the cause of infection, and the outbreaks of fever continued.

Throughout the first two months, the Spirit of God would supernaturally give me questions to ask. They were the kind of questions one would need some medical knowledge or training to know how and what to ask. But God did that for me. He presented me to the doctors as someone who was willing to speak with them according to the stance of faith I had taken, yet who also possessed a respectable measure of intelligence about the situation. I became someone to be reckoned with regarding the care of my child, and it was all by the Spirit of God.

The Holy Spirit made me aware of things I wouldn't normally be aware of—bits of information necessary to know about for Christina's survival, because something always seemed to pop up in an attempt to take her life. Everything from high fevers and organ malfunction to breathing difficulties and heart irregularities tried to end her life at the most unexpected times. Nevertheless, Christina continued to live.

Finally one day the hospital neurosurgeon came to us and said we needed to institutionalize Christina. Since she was classified as a PVS (persistent vegetative state), they accepted that it would be Christina's permanent state and expected Nick and me to do likewise. But Nick and I didn't agree with that prognosis. Even though we had nothing to go on other than what God had spoken to my heart, that was enough.

The time had come for us to make some serious, significant changes concerning Christina. Although the hospital was telling us to institutionalize her—and they offered us no alternatives—we did not agree. Nick and I knew we needed to send her to a rehabilitation facility that specialized in coma intervention.

Nick's medical knowledge gave him a platform for research as he searched to locate the best hospitals. At times, I was thoroughly awed by my husband's persistence. Despite all his logic, rationality, and medical knowledge of what we faced in that situation, despite all the conflicting advice we were getting, Nick made some phenomenal choices to pursue what others had said was improbable or impossible: the awakening of Christina.

Nick went about the laborious task of seeking a rehabilitation center somewhere in the United States that would accept a patient who was still comatose and requiring life-supporting oxygen. (Very few will.) He researched until he found the names of the three leading facilities. Nick contacted them and set up appointments for us to meet the directors of hospitals in Chicago, Houston, and Washington, D. C., which offered rehabilitation facilities specializing in coma treatment. He wanted to talk to the directors of these institutions and study the papers they had written in the area of their expertise concerning coma care and treatment.

Nick and I planned to fly into each city, meet the hospital director and staff, take a tour of their facilities, and then fly back out the same day. Each time, Nick made arrangements for Christina to be cared for by special private-care nurses. He provided someone to be with her around the clock to keep her and her bedding clean. She was constantly in clean gowns and washed. Nick could have relied on the hospital nurses to care for Christina, but he knew they wouldn't have enough time to tend to her with the frequency he preferred. Nick did everything possible to keep the atmosphere bright and alive around Christina.

In our absence, we also had family and friends who stayed with Christina; many were believers who knew how to hear from and respond to the Holy Spirit. We wanted to be certain she was cared for both naturally and spiritually. In the battle we faced contending for Christina's life, the severity of the natural circumstances could not be ignored. But neither could we ignore the intensity of the struggle in the spirit. Therefore, we made sure we had covered all our bases.

After we flew to all three hospitals, Nick and I decided to take Christina to the rehabilitation hospital in Houston, the largest medical center in the world. Nick was pleased when he read the research papers of the doctors there. We also liked the Houston doctors once we had the opportunity to speak to them. In addition, Nick had a strong gut feeling that Houston was the right place.

Most families don't want to venture beyond their own geographic region for this type of care because of the distance. But no region was too far for Nick. He was determined to take his child where she could receive the best care.

It seemed that perhaps the Washington, D. C., location would have been better suited for us since we had family and friends in that city. Nick also had colleagues and friends in Chicago who could have stepped in to help us if needed. We didn't know a soul in Houston; nevertheless, we both knew that Houston was the best choice for Christina.

The hospital, however, disagreed with our decision to move Christina to a rehabilitation facility. Apparently, they viewed our response to their insistence to institutionalize Christina as either foolhardy or ill advised. I'm not sure which. But because the hospital did not recommend or support our decision to move Christina, the insurance company refused to support the cost of transporting her from Nashville to Houston by jet.

The hospital staff was amazed that she had lived so long. They couldn't explain how or why she had managed to survive the horrible trauma she endured. They tolerated our expressions of faith and allowed our additional support staff of nurses and praying friends to aid us in our daily vigils. The hospital staff was very kind as they accommodated the sweeping entourage of friends, family, and media that followed us during the first weeks after Christina's accident. But now the novelty was over. We were months into a situation that remained without change.

I suppose we couldn't really blame the doctors for the stance they held. They had seen countless situations before that bore close resemblance to what we faced with Christina: a brain-damaged comatose patient who continues, for whatever reason, to live against the odds. Those situations all concluded with the patient being institutionalized. Based on their experience and expectation, our situation was no different. And our refusal to accept the limitations of their experience and expectations as somehow definitive for our own cut a gaping gulf of ideological differences between us.

While the hospital staff provided the best care possible for Christina, they still expected her to die or, at best, to live the lifeless existence of a human vegetable. We, on the other hand, expected Christina not only to live, but also to be fully restored to a vibrant life of wholeness. What was the basis for this vast difference in our expectation? *God said so.*

Against this background of negative expectations, there was always one doctor who fought hard for Christina both medically and with hope, her trauma surgeon, Dr. Ed. He had brought her through her devastating injuries. When others challenged the soundness of our plans, he spoke up on our behalf to the others and said, "Christina is so young. Give her a chance."

Once we took the final steps to move Christina to Houston, everything fell quickly into place. Nick arranged to charter a jet and secure flight paramedics and nurses to care for Christina during our flight to Houston.

The morning of the move, a nurse from trauma nursing care came into Christina's room, where I sat waiting for Nick to finalize the release papers. Speaking in a voice resonating with deep concern, he looked down at Christina lying in the contorted posture we viewed daily and said, "You know, Mrs. Varallo, what you're about to do is probably the worst decision you could make concerning your daughter because it will change nothing. This is as good as it gets for Christina. A rehabilitation hospital will not alter her condition in the least. What you see right now is what you will see for the rest of her life. Accept it. This is as good as it gets."

I don't think his words could possibly be more opposed strategically to all that was in my heart at that moment. Sitting there at the bedside of my comatose daughter, preparing to take a huge leap of faith in the direction of her miracle, I was struggling against my own internal questions about what to expect next. I was convinced that we were taking the right step and that Houston was the right facility. But was there perhaps something I hadn't considered?

It seemed as though every time we caught our breath where Christina was concerned, something else completely unexpected would come along and knock the wind out of us. Surely, I hoped, we were past that now. But how could I prepare for the unknown? The last thing I needed to hear were words so doubt-filled that they challenged my stance and clawed aggressively at my resolve.

"You do realize that, don't you, Mrs. Varallo?" He repeated, "This is as good as it gets for Christina."

Standing up to turn toward him, I replied, "I realize that Christina has been classified as PVS (persistent vegetative state), but we do expect a better outcome for her." I kept my voice steady, pleasant, without edginess but firm. As we stood there looking at one another, the dividing lines were clearly drawn. The knot in my stomach tightened as Nick walked in to announce, "The papers are signed. The ambulance is downstairs. We're ready to go."

The nurse shrugged his shoulders and walked out. That was it. Now that we were officially released from the hospital, we were on our own. Literally.

The paramedic team we hired had arrived. They would assist us, if needed, in the ambulance and on the jet flight to Houston. They disconnected Christina from the hospital equipment, hooked up an oxygen bottle to her trachea, and eased her onto the stretcher. Nick and I followed closely behind the team as they maneuvered Christina into the freight elevator. My heart was pounding a bit as we exited onto the first floor. So many times I had imagined the day when we would bring Christina home from the hospital. This in no way resembled what I had envisioned.

As we turned the corner, I was startled by shouts from several people running in from the parking lot, waving wildly in our direction. Outside in the distance, I could hear the blare of sirens and a trumpeting car horn that sounded like a disturbed safety alarm. Suddenly a hospital alarm went off, filling the corridor with deafening blasts that almost certainly were a warning code of some impending danger.

Amidst all the people shouting and running and the combined scream of the sirens, horns, and alarms, pandemonium rushed in like a coastal storm as waves of panic swept over us all.

"Nick," I called out, "what's going on?"

His expression looked stunned. "Something's on fire."

About that time, a man rushed up with both arms flailing. "Your ambulance is on fire!" he exclaimed. "You can't go out there."

We froze.

I couldn't believe it. For the past two months, almost daily we were confronted by a physical emergency of some kind that threatened Christina's life and safety.

Now this obvious, nearly absurd attack of the enemy was launched against us to prevent the move we were about to make. Our first aggressive step of faith had detonated a land mine of resistance. We couldn't retreat; there was no place to go. We had to move forward toward our hope of Christina's restoration. But at every turn, including this current challenge, we kept hitting barriers that backed us into a corner, requiring a miracle to help us go over, around, or through it.

How many more brick walls will we have to scale? I wondered.

Speak to the mountain and keep moving, I heard the Holy One say. *Don't cower now. This is not a sign that you aren't supposed to move her. I said life and wholeness. Now keep moving!* The authority in His voice as He spoke to my heart drenched me with peace, and I was engulfed by a sense of His nearness.

The flight paramedic who noticed the signal that Christina's oxygen bottle was nearly empty interrupted my thoughts. "This bottle's almost gone! Where's your oxygen?" the flight paramedic demanded, his voice betraying the panic his expression sought to conceal.

The ambulance attendant's face went pale. "My extra oxygen is out there," he said, motioning toward our ambulance with its engine on fire. "Where's the emergency room?" someone in our group shouted.

No one knew. None of us was familiar with this section of the hospital. Suddenly a tall man appeared at the end of the long corridor and said to us, "Go to your right, down that way. Then pass through the set of doors to your left. You'll find the emergency room." All of us took hold of the gurney supporting Christina's stretcher and began to run in the direction where the man was pointing.

By this time Christina was choking, making deep gurgling sounds. She was drowning in her own phlegm. We burst into the emergency room, shouting, "We need oxygen! We need suction!"

Startled by our unauthorized presence, the emergency room staff blocked us, demanding, "Who are you? What's your authority to enter here?" Our team was moving quickly, pushing past them as though they fully intended to find what they needed on their own, when suddenly a woman stood in front of us. Pointing her finger at me, she said, "I know you. Follow me." She led us into a room that had everything Christina needed. Immediately, our medical team started suction and hooked her up to a new oxygen bottle. I turned to look for the woman who brought us into the room, but she was gone. I had no clue who that woman was. I had never seen her before in my life. But if she knew me, I was relieved for the favor that gave us access.

We'd need all the favor we could get before that day would end.

Immediately after Christina received the oxygen and care she needed, we loaded her into another ambulance that had been sent to carry us to the plane, which by now had been waiting on us for two hours.

When we arrived at the private airport, my dearest friend, Karen Mosely, was there waiting for me. We spent a few moments together. "Karen," I said, "I can't believe we are doing this, going to Texas. I thought when we left the hospital we would be taking Christina home and out of a coma—not this way!" Karen and I were not just dearest of friends, but prayer partners too. She also had been at the hospital every day watching and praying. And now I was leaving for Texas.

Karen has always had the right words. She hugged me, then took my hand and said, "Mary Fran, you know God, you know His voice, your hand is in His, and He will continue to lead you." With that, Nick and I boarded the jet, and we began our journey to Houston, Texas.

After we were settled in the small jet, the pilot assured us we'd be in Houston within an hour. The jet was barely off the ground, however, when Christina went into crisis again. Her breathing became extremely shallow, her heart rate was pounding out of control, and her blood pressure was skyrocketing. It was so unbelievably high that we wondered why the little arrow didn't spin off the dial! No matter what the emergency personnel did for her, she wasn't taking in enough oxygen. Hovering at 40,000 feet in the air above Houston, we were losing Christina.

"How much longer do we have before we land?" our paramedic called out to the pilot.

"We should have been ready for descent by now, but we're backed up behind two planes. We don't have clearance to land, so it's going to be another twenty minutes or so."

"We don't have twenty minutes!" the medic shouted. "She's slipping!"

The plane was not a medic-flight; therefore, we could not request medical clearance with the air traffic controller. Furthermore, the only emergency supplies available were what our team had brought.

The thought of hovering for an additional twenty minutes made my heart sink. The blur of motion around me seemed surreal, as if I were watching it all while detached from my own body. In my mind, I could see the face of the nurse from the hospital, his lips moving in slow motion as he repeated the words, "You know, Mrs. Varallo, this is probably the worst possible thing you could do for Christina."

The worst thing...the worst thing...the worst.... The words echoed mockingly through my thoughts. No one in the hospital believed we were doing the right thing. No one supported our decision. We hadn't even made it out of the hospital without Christina going into crisis. Now it appeared as though she was failing. Is this how it all would end? At every bend, with every alarming attack, divine intervention had brought us through. Surely God hadn't brought us this far only to let Christina die suspended between earth and sky!

A row of seats had been moved out to accommodate the stretcher. The already-small jet was now very tight quarters. I slipped out of the way while Nick moved in closer to Christina to work with the medics, who were each focusing on something different as they tried desperately to stabilize Christina's vital signs.

As I inched over toward the front of the plane, I looked back over my shoulder to see Nick reach over to Christina. Patting her arm gently, he called to her, "Christina, honey, hang in there. Hold on...." The sight of Nick's slender 6' 3" frame crouched down to softly cradle Christina's head with the awkward tenderness of a father holding his newborn was an image that bore down deep into me.

I slumped into a seat, pressed my nose against the glass, and cried as I prayed, "Father, it's been almost two months now. You know what? This is getting really hard."

The pilot and the medical team were shouting information back and forth, but I couldn't understand what they were saying. The muffled sound of my own sobs drowned them out.

"Father," I continued to pray, the salty taste of my own tears coursing across my lips, "we are so close...so close. Somehow, You're going to have to step in and help us land. You've got to get us on the ground. Here we are again in an impossible situation, but *You* said 'life and wholeness,' and I believe You."

'Control, we've got a medical emergency on board...."

The pilot was talking to the tower, explaining our situation. I gathered from the discussion that one of the airline planes ahead of us would have to back out in order for us to gain clearance to pass through and land.

"Her temperature is reading 104 degrees! She can't hold on much longer!" one of the medics said.

"Hang on, Christina. You can make it."

Everyone was talking—to each other, to themselves, to Christina. The whirring sound of words coming from every direction was suddenly stilled when the pilot said, "We're getting clearance to land!"

"...and tell them we wish them all our best!" called out a voice from the control tower through the monitor.

Clearance came so quickly, the pilot dropped the nose of the plane like a fighter jet and dove into Houston. An ambulance and a medical crew were waiting for us on the runway. Everyone began working feverishly with Christina because they were losing her vital signs. The flurry of all the commotion was maddening. A car was waiting to take Nick and me with the ambulance to the hospital.

Speeding closely behind the ambulance, racing through traffic and against the clock, Nick and I were crying, clinging to hope as we clutched each other's hand. "Honey," Nick said, staring at the scene before us, "I hope we've made the right decision."

"Nick," I sputtered through tears, "I know we did the right thing. Believe me, we did the right thing." I repeated the words to settle my own soul as much as to settle his.

Navigating the circuitous route from the airport to the hospital while trying to keep up with the ambulance was a challenge. We didn't know where we were. Houston was totally unfamiliar to us. The hospital, which had been alerted to our arrival, was also unfamiliar. So much was completely unknown. But although so much about our future and Christina's future felt tentative and unknown, the Hand that guided us and held us safe was familiar, and His goodness was surely known—even amidst the terror of this situation.

My thoughts were darting around as quickly as the ambulance that sped down the highway in front of us. Nick and I stared at the small back window, straining to catch at least a glimpse of all the activity that was aimed at keeping Christina alive. Perhaps we thought that if we could just keep our eyes focused on her, our very determination might will her to hold on and fight.

"Christina, hang in there, honey," Nick whispered.

"Father, give them wisdom," I prayed, thinking of the medical team working feverishly to save her. In the crisis of the moment, any and every procedure could cast the deciding call between life and death.

With a jolt, the car slammed to a stop, jarring me to notice that we'd pulled into the parking lot of Tirr Hospital of Houston Medical Center. Almost before it came to a complete stop, the ambulance door swung open and the team spilled out, pulling Christina's stretcher out and onto a waiting gurney in one swift move. They barely noticed our approach as we ran over to the ambulance. Trying to catch my breath, I asked a paramedic, "How's she doing?"

His face flushed, the paramedic turned and called out to me as he ran through the emergency entrance door: "She made it here, but all her vitals are out of control. If you believe in miracles, you'd better start praying for one!"

The Holy Spirit Provides Wisdom

I have always been fascinated by the way the Holy Spirit will suddenly inform me of things I know absolutely nothing about. That was the case in this chapter when I shared with you how He gave me knowledge of specific medical terminology so I could ask the medical teams attending Christina the right questions. This is such an amazing gift when you stop to think about it.

Sometimes I think we forget that the Holy Spirit is God. And because He is God, the Holy Spirit is all knowing. If we will learn to distinguish His voice from our own thoughts and from other voices, we will be amazed by all He wants to share with us about our lives. He will even give us knowledge of certain things that are about to be, because Jesus said He would lead and guide us into all truth and show us things to come. (John 16:13-15.) What truth has God revealed to you recently?

The Holy Spirit speaks of our future as though it already was because He's already been there. He also speaks of a way prepared by Him for us in the days ahead that will be waiting for us upon our arrival.

Journal

_____

_____

_____

_____

_____

_____

_____

_____

_____

_____

_____

_____

_____

_____

_____

_____

7

Having Done All–Stand!

*"And whatsoever ye shall ask in my name, that will
I do, that the Father may be glorified in the Son.
If ye shall ask any thing in my name, I will do it."*

JOHN 14:13,14

Inside the hospital, the respiratory team flanked
Christina, everyone working quickly in their respective
roles. Then Dr. Kathryn Bonke, the hospital director with
whom we'd spoken several times but had never met, came
in to join her medical team as they worked on Christina.
Dr. Bonke was one of the primary reasons we had come
to Houston, and our faith in her was well rewarded.

By this time, Christina's fever registered 105 degrees. As part of the medical team concentrated on trying to stabilize her heart rate and bring her blood pressure down, a respiratory therapist got ready to suction Christina's airway so she could take in more oxygen.

When I saw them getting ready to suction her, I shouted, "Wait! You need to know what happens to her when you do that!"

Immediately the respiratory therapist spun around and stared at me. "What do you mean? What do you know?" he snapped.

Before I could reply, Dr. Bonke saw my expression, stepped forward, and said to her team, "Pay attention to her. She's the girl's mother. She's been with her when this happened before." With that said, they were willing to listen to me.

Christina would go into bronchial spasms when suctioned, which shut down her oxygen supply. The medical staff then had to work and force her bronchials open, and the only way to open her air passages was to Ambu bag her. This had been an ongoing problem.

But by the time they performed the suction procedure, Christina's levels were dropping rapidly. Nothing was working to provoke the needed response. She'd gone too long without oxygen. Once again Christina was in a crisis threatening her life. The oxygen therapist alerted Dr. Bonke that her levels were dropping and there was no response. Then Dr. Bonke shouted, "Bag her, bag her again!"

I stepped out of the room. Of course, everyone thought I had left because I was upset. And I was. Who wouldn't be at the sight and sound of it all? But deeper than the pain I felt from watching my daughter go through this was the anger and weariness I felt from our constant contending against the unrelenting barrage of adversarial attacks that challenged God's plan for her life. This entire ordeal had stretched out into an experience I never could have imagined.

I needed to go somewhere—*anywhere*—so I could be alone to pray. At that moment, I could barely breathe. I didn't know what to say or how to pray any differently than I had before. God had spoken, and that was what I believed. I had already marked my line in the sand. Now the only thing left for me to do was to stand there and trust in His faithfulness to perform His Word.

Then just outside the room I found a quiet corner by a window where I could remind both God and myself of what He had said. I paced and I prayed. I prayed for the doctors. I prayed for anyone and everyone attending Christina at that moment. I prayed for Nick. I prayed for me. I prayed, *Father, You are the God of my childhood. I have no reason to doubt You. I have chosen to believe it is life and wholeness for Christina.*

What else remained? What else could be done? I wondered.

Blanketing the situation in prayer clothed my own emotions with the confidence only the hand of God can bestow. As I had many times before, I wondered how anyone could even attempt to walk through a normal day—let alone pass through the rigors of life—without a conscious awareness of the Spirit of God.

So many times we have read the passage in the twenty-third Psalm that says God prepares a table before us in the presence of our enemies and anoints our head with oil until our cup runs over. But how many times have we read those verses without understanding that they describe God's response to us when we must confront our "enemies"—fear, sickness, or stress?

I am continually grateful for the privilege given to every believer in Jesus Christ of slipping into that secret place of God's presence, guided by the Holy Spirit. When we are bombarded by the unrelenting shouts of disturbing facts, God will always speak truth. In the stillness of that revelation, there is calm—and the facts can be forced to conform to His truth.

I returned to find Christina stabilized and Nick talking with the doctors. Now that they had been "introduced" to Christina, a few things needed to be discussed concerning her care. The matter of her frequent bouts with a high fever continued to be a source of concern. I left them to continue their conversation.

So here we were, transplanted in a matter of a few hours from the friendly confines of home and the wonderful support of family and friends to the unknown world of a hospital in Houston with our miracle in waiting.

Nick's sister Frances Anne had flown in just hours before our arrival and had begun the process of finding a furnished apartment for me. She also contacted Barbara, who was the sister of a dear friend. Together they met us at the hospital.

In the course of a few days, we secured an apartment, got me settled in, and then Nick and Frances Anne flew back to Nashville.

The vigil continued, and I returned to the same routine for this phase of Christina's recovery that I had followed since the beginning.

Steered by a Steady Hand

Every morning I awakened early to spend time with the Holy Spirit, entering into the presence of the Lord while reading His Word. Most of the time I would simply speak to Him out of my heart, telling Him how much I loved Him, telling Him how thankful I was for His love for me, for my daughter, for my family. I'd tell Him how much I trusted His plan and His provision for me. Sometimes He would tell me something specific to pray about for Christina, for the doctors, or for something else.

When we don't know what to do or what to pray, God tells us. I can think of nothing more comforting than the realization that it is possible to be steered by a steady Hand through the turbulent circumstances of life.

As sons and daughters of God the Father, the Spirit of God can lead us just as Jesus was led through every situation. If we will simply pay attention to the Holy Spirit and obey Him, we don't have to be taken by surprise or reduced to failure through ignorance.

Throughout the entire ordeal with Christina, I was most grateful for the way the Holy Spirit led me in prayer when I did not know what to pray. He would also tell me what to do or say in agreement with the Scriptures.

Speak to the Mountain

One morning well into the second week after we had moved Christina to Houston, I was brushing my teeth when the Holy Spirit spoke to my heart, *Look over there to the left.*

When I glanced up into the mirror, my eyes were opened to see into the realm of the spirit as though it were actually before me. In this small vision, I saw a mountain. As I looked at it, I heard the Holy Spirit say, *That mountain represents Christina's fevers that the doctors have not been able to stop. Speak to it and tell it to leave now.* So, I did exactly that.

I said, "You mountain of fever, in the name of Jesus, be gone!"

Then I heard the Holy Spirit say, *Now, watch.* As I looked, suddenly that mountain just disappeared as though it had exploded and been whisked off the horizon.

As I watched, I was reminded of what Jesus said: If we have faith the size of a grain of mustard seed, we can speak to a mountain and it will be thrown into the sea. (Matthew 17:20; Matthew 21:21; Mark 11:23.)

That very day when I went to the hospital, I learned that Christina's fever had escalated during the night. The doctors told me there was a chance she needed to be moved out of their rehabilitation facility into an acute care hospital because she was too ill from fevers they just could not control.

When I walked into the room, the first thing I noticed was the ultra-modern, space-age-looking, computerized equipment surrounding Christina. They had placed her on a special cooling mattress with a blanket designed to help regulate her body temperature.

A doctor was there with her, checking her levels and discussing something with the attending nurse. When he saw me, the doctor began explaining what was going on with Christina and his great concern. He also described the measures they were taking to reduce her fever—but to no avail. Nothing was working.

However, the image of that mountain God showed me just hours ago was still very vivid to me. I knew God had instructed me to speak to the fever and command it to go. We would have to see the results at some point. I just knew it.

While I listened to the doctor's explanations of why it was so critical for Christina's fever to break soon, her temperature level suddenly dropped straight down to normal while we watched. It was phenomenal. Actually, it was *impossible* for her temperature to drop that drastically and quickly from 103 degrees to 98.6 degrees without her body going into convulsions.

The doctor just stared with incredulity at the monitoring equipment. Then he began to scurry around, checking the machine to be certain it was functioning properly.

God had obliterated the fever that morning when He told me to speak to the mountain. Because He initiated that act by showing me the mountain in a vision and by telling me what to say, I came into Christina's room confident that He had already settled the matter.

The Command of Faith

At times, Christians want to give the command of authority in a situation simply because it worked for them previously by faith in another situation. But one cannot truly give the command of faith apart from the inspiration of the Spirit of God.

It is not necessary to have a vision before dealing with a matter in the spirit. But it is necessary to be *in* the spirit to be able to respond *by* the Spirit in a situation. The command of faith is to rise out of the overflow supply of the Spirit in our hearts—the fruit of our daily fellowship with Him. Yes, there are times when He will come upon us in the gift of faith to speak something into or out of existence; but for that command to be effective, it must be initiated by the Spirit, not just the result of uninspired dead works.

It is an insult to the Father God for us to attempt to "work the Word" apart from the specific guidance and direction He ordained to give us through the Person of the Holy Spirit. God's plan for us has always been that we experience a vital, active, and real union with Him through daily fellowship.

God is so aware of our specific and daily needs. Jesus even instructed us to ask the Father for our "daily" bread. The Holy Spirit is ever present to guide us into the truth that will trigger our deliverance or provision in any given situation on a daily basis—*if* we will listen and obey what He tells us.

Neither listening to the Holy Spirit without acting, nor acting without listening to Him will produce the desired results. So many times people do not achieve the outcome they hope for after making their confessions and expecting things to change simply because *they did not allow the Holy One to guide them in what to confess* or what to expect.

Yes, every word of God is alive and productive. *But the Spirit of Truth is so precise; He will lead you to speak precisely what is needed according to the root of the matter.* And many times the deep, underlying issue He is choosing to address is completely unknown to you but known to Him.

'This Is Like a Nightmare!'

I didn't know how long we'd need to be in Houston. But we had prepared for the long haul even as we kept expecting this awful waiting period to end. That's how I viewed it all. I was waiting for God's promise concerning Christina to come to pass. What her doctors defined as her final state was, in my eyes, just a phase until her passage into recovery was complete.

Our stay in Houston had now been two weeks. Nick was coming to Houston that weekend, as usual. I looked forward to his visit. From the start, Nick had been a pillar we had all leaned on in certain ways. His strength was such a support to all of us. His clear-headed logic and reason brought a stabilizing brace and balance. And for me, it was a great comfort.

When Nick arrived that weekend, he came into Christina's room, where he knew I would be. "I can't tell you what it was like driving into the hospital tonight from the airport," he said. "This is like a nightmare. I don't even know what I'm doing here! It's been too long, Mary Fran. This has gone on way too long."

We just stared at each other. I was stunned beyond comprehension by his words. For the first time in a while, I really looked at Nick. I had been so consumed with Christina and our battle for her life that I hadn't noticed the toll the struggle had taken on others—especially Nick.

Nick had held on to the hope of Christina's recovery, hoping for everything that neither her physical condition nor his medical training could lead him to expect. Nick had pressed past all that he saw physically and knew to be true medically. He had stood firm with me, resisting any and all who would resist us in our quest to ride out the tide and beat the odds.

Nick had done everything humanly, medically, and financially possible to surround Christina with anything that was conducive to life and recovery—all because he wanted the best for her and he believed me when I told him that God had spoken to me the words "life and wholeness for Christina." By believing the words I told him God had spoken to my heart, Nick, in fact, believed God too. But now he was tired. Tired beyond reason. Tired beyond endurance. And he was scared. So was I— now more than ever.

My heart went out to him. My eyes implored him, but I just couldn't respond. The words wouldn't come. All I could do was take his hand, clasping it between mine as we stood there, burdened beneath the accumulated pressure of all we felt, all we had shoved down for two months. At that moment, it felt unbearable. Still without exchanging words, we turned to go downstairs to get something to eat.

As we walked through the hospital, a beautiful young girl passed by us accompanied by her parents. As the girl supported herself somewhat awkwardly with crutches, we could see that she was actually laboring to balance herself on two artificial legs.

"I'd rather Christina was like that than the way she is now," Nick said.

"What do you mean?" I asked as I spun around to face him. "I don't want Christina like that. I want her whole!"

Nick's dark eyes looked straight through me when he said, "We might need to consider lifting the code on Christina to revive her if her heart stops or if she stops breathing again."

"Nick," I nearly shouted, "you can't be serious!"

"The way Christina is now is not really living," Nick said. "What good has it done to bring her back only to return to that state, barely existing? I want more for her than that kind of torture! We at least need to think about the other alternative."

"We can't think that way. We won't think that way!"

I don't know what was said in conversation after that. My head was reeling. Previously, every time we were besieged with a barrage of words calling for us to give up and give in, Nick and I were always on the same side, wielding our unified defense against an external attack. But this—this was different.

Weariness was now trying to drive a wedge between us. I couldn't bear the thought of it! Too many thoughts and questions collided in my mind. Would I now have to stand against Nick, too, until the change came? Could it possibly come to that? Surely not!

Could it?

That night back at the apartment, Nick and I were preoccupied by our own thoughts. Emotionally, both of us were chaffing against any remaining restraint, groping in our individual struggles to make sense of the mayhem that for two months now had consumed every aspect of our lives.

The next day, we were scheduled to meet with the Houston medical team to discuss Christina. Whether or not we were to continue full code and life support on her was almost certain to come up in the conversation. What would Nick say? What would I do? The weighty anticipation of so many dreaded "what ifs" pressed heavily against my mind and my emotions.

We need to consider taking the code off Christina.

We need to at least consider that alternative, Mary Fran.

The words still hung hauntingly in the air. For the first time in two months, sleep eluded me.

The Crucial Decision

"Dr. Varallo, do you still want to maintain a full code on Christina if she should experience cardiac or respiratory arrest?"

In our meeting with the team of specialists, the dreaded question entered the discussion early on the agenda of topics.

Nick did not respond right away. The doctor did not press for an immediate reply. She waited, leaving her question suspended, dangling before us to ponder as we considered the finality of its consequences.

I held my breath.

The silence only accentuated the size of the conference room where we now met with the team assigned to Christina's case. The way our chairs were positioned at the table, my back was toward Nick. I could not see his face, and I was almost grateful that he could not see the single tear that spilled down mine.

I felt every muscle in my body tense. My mind raced as I wondered what Nick would say; what I could do if he said no code; what it would mean if we did not agree; what if...

"Yes..."

What? What did he say? Nick's words jerked me out of my own mental conversation, back into the discussion at hand.

"Yes," Nick repeated. "Keep the full code on Christina."

I nearly fainted from relief. Somehow, God had gotten to Nick's heart during the night!

Oh, Father, thank You! I thank You! I prayed silently.

My heart was pounding so fiercely that I could feel the pulsation of my own blood flow throbbing in my ears, even my fingertips. My entire system was in shock, much like the stunned consciousness of a person who narrowly escaped catastrophe. Other decisions were made regarding Christina at that meeting, but I was only vaguely aware of what was being discussed. Then it was over, and it was time for Nick to return to Nashville.

As he drove me to the apartment, we didn't discuss why he kept Christina on full code. Our emotions were shot, scraped raw from repeated run-ins with death and impossibilities on a daily basis over the past few months. I felt myself crumbling inside. Nick was right. This had gone on too long.

Our nerves were frayed. We'd done all we could do. We'd stood. And stood. And stood.... We'd held on to God's words. There were even moments when we distinctly felt God's words holding onto us, keeping us from dismantling when the pressure was so great.

But the pressure had never been greater than at this moment. This pressure was countered by the mounting hysteria I felt inside. It was as if the muffled sound of my own soul, gagged and kicking, kept echoing inside my brain.

After Nick brought me to our tiny, temporary Houston apartment, we exchanged information and a difficult good-bye, and then he drove himself to the airport to fly back to Nashville. And I was alone.

Alone–But Never Alone

I don't know how long I stood by the window crying, staring into the distance, mulling over the jumbled quagmire that had become our lives. Everything seemed to fall on one side or the other of that defining, dividing line: *The Accident.*

I thought of Christina and Nicholas as children. They were both so beautiful and smart. Nick and I adored them. As they grew and developed in their own individual interests and talents, we were so proud of them. I recalled the last time I saw Christina before the accident, replaying our conversation in my mind. Almost intrusively, another memory came to mind—the morning the church secretary called to say Christina had been in an accident. Then I remembered Nick's words to me that weekend:

It's been too long, Mary Fran. We might need to start thinking about other alternatives. I winced as the words bit even harder, deeper than before. I couldn't bear the thought of Nick and I standing at opposite ends concerning Christina. We both only wanted what was best for her; I knew that. Nick took such pride in Christina's athletic abilities and free-spirited nature. He was even proud of her strong, independent streak—whether he would admit it or not.

Nick could not bare the thought of seeing Christina trapped inside a shattered, motionless body. I understand what he felt, but I could not—would not—surrender to lifelessness as her final outcome. And I could not bear the thought of Nick and me wanting the same thing for Christina yet considering it in different ways. No! This battle was difficult enough; I could not handle an emotional tug of war, too, in addition to everything else.

So many losses... I thought.

My daughter was trapped in a coma. My family was turned upside down by the event and the continuing saga of it. And now, I seemed to be losing Nick's support.

Suddenly, all the emotion I had stuffed and shoved deep down inside erupted to the surface.

"ABBA! GOD! MY FATHER!"

I was startled by the piercing wail of a horrible, tortured scream. I was even more stunned when I recognized the mournful cry as my own! I stood in the middle of the room and screamed as long and loud as I could into the pillow I had lifted from the couch. I screamed over and over and over—until I was empty.

Gulping between sobs, I shouted, "God, I don't know what we're going to do about this. This is getting to be too much. You've heard all that's been said, and You see all that's going on. Now, I don't know the plan for Your manifestation of Christina's healing, but I cannot go another day! I tell You, I *cannot* go another day. I'm real sorry if there's some reason You wanted the manifestation to come a different way, but I am telling You, I cannot go another day. Father, I can't do it.

"So whatever Your plan is, can we have an alternative? Would You just get this thing manifested, because *I cannot go through this another day!*"

He Will Be With You

In this chapter, I shared the experience of a very hard time that my husband, Nick, and I went through. You may be experiencing a time such as that, when there simply are not enough words left inside you from which you can gather strength—not enough words through which you can express yourself to be understood.

Sometimes I think I become wordless, feeling as though I no longer even know the right words to affect or change something. But I can assure you that when or if you were to experience such a time, the Holy Spirit would be with you. He will take hold of you and give you what you must have in that moment, whether it be the words to speak or the confidence you need to have in Him—in what God the Father has said and in what Jesus gave His life to provide.

You and I may be without words, but the Father and His Son are not. And out of Their love for you, the Holy Spirit, Who abides with you forever, will get you through that moment in that particular space of time, just as He did for me. You can trust Him because you have made a decision to know Him as you have never known Him before. Take a moment and reflect on some experiences that you are going through. You can use the lines below to express your feelings and thoughts. What is God speaking to you about this experience? What words is He giving to you? How are you finding comfort knowing that He will always be with you?

Journal

Journal

_____

_____

_____

_____

_____

_____

_____

_____

_____

_____

_____

_____

_____

_____

_____

_____

8

Suddenly...

"[God's words] are life to those who find them,
and health to all their flesh."

PROVERBS 4:22 NKJV

I sat there sobbing into the pillow until my chest ached
and I could barely breathe. My eyes were swollen shut.
I felt drained and completely numb.

Clutching the pillow to me tightly, I rocked back
and forth, settling myself in the silence of the now
darkened apartment.

"Father," I prayed, "I don't know what else to ask You other than what I've already said. So I'm just going to sit here, sing to You, tell You that I love You, and worship You."

The Peace and Power of Worship

When all else seemed to be stripped away, when nothing or no one else was in view, there was one thing I yet possessed—my fellowship with God. When all I thought I knew seemed pointless, when all I attempted to do seemed fruitless, worship would take me to a place in Him where peace prevailed over the tumult of my inner storm. Regardless of what I did or did not understand, I could quiet my heart with one truth: He is worthy. God is worthy of my praise, worthy of my adoration, worthy of my love because He is still God. And He is greater than pain I cannot endure. Even in the midst of my darkest moments, His light surrounds me.

"One thing have I desired of You, my Lord," I whispered, "this and this only will I seek after—that I may dwell in Your presence, Holy One, all the days of my life. I want to see only Your beauty."

Then I began to sing to the Lord in the singsong cadence of a small child: "I love You, Lord. Holy One, to me, You are wonderful. You are my peace. My life You keep. Always the same. Always so near. When I cry. When I feel fear. You are still with me. You hold my hand. You help me stand. I love You, my Lord, my wonderful Friend."

On and on, I sang my simple expressions of devotion to Him. I sensed the warmth of His presence envelop me as I poured out my heart to Him in song.

Mine is not a beautiful voice. I am sure that no human ears would have enjoyed my song. But my Father God took delight in me as I sang to Him that night, as He does in us all when we express to Him our love.

In the stillness of that time with Him, my heart gained new strength when His everlasting arms lifted me into a place of peace. In that place, alone with Him, I could say with the psalmist, *"He maketh me to lie down in green pastures: he leadeth me beside the still waters. He restoreth my soul..."* (Psalm 23:2,3).

Weeping May Endure for a Night, but...

In the morning, I awakened rested and settled. But before I even got out of bed, I heard the voice of the Holy Spirit tell me to speak to the bronchial spasms Christina would have.

"Speak to it and tell it, *No more!*"

It wasn't as though I hadn't been praying and believing for this to stop. But His command was absolute. So I said, "Yes, Sir!" and I spoke to it exactly as He told me to do. Then I continued to prepare for my day at the hospital.

Each day I would read healing Scriptures over Christina. That particular day I brought with me a small book written by Charles Capps entitled *God's Creative Power for Healing.* A nurse was always present in the room with Christina because of her need for constant care. The nurse sitting with her that particular afternoon had been with her many times before. She had seen me reading the Bible to Christina and had heard me each time I spoke to Christina's spirit and commanded her body to come in line with God's promise. The nurse never interrupted me, nor did she make any comment.

That afternoon was no different.

After reading to Christina as I usually did, I walked over to her and kissed her. I looked at her bent arms and tightly curled hands that bore more resemblance to bird wings than human appendages. Her neck bent down, cocking her head awkwardly to the left. A pool of saliva collected under her chin and trickled over the thin film capping the trachea that created an airway for her. I smoothed the rumpled sheets to conceal the area exposed when her diaper and bed sheets were changed. Bending down to her ear, I placed my hands on Christina and said, "Now, body, you listen to me. This is what God's Word says about you. You've heard me before; hear me now again. Hear me one more time."

I didn't know what the nurse thought about my words and actions, but I didn't really care either. After speaking to Christina's body, I sat back down and continued to read the Bible. But in a matter of minutes, the nurse stood up and shouted to me excitedly, "Look!"

I leapt to my feet, rushing over to join her at Christina's bedside. We looked in stunned amazement at what was taking place before our eyes.

Suddenly, Christina's face had begun to change.

The muscles in her face relaxed from their contorted position. Her head, which was always drooped and stuck to one side, was released and lifted. The nonstop stream of drool pouring from her mouth suddenly stopped.

Suddenly...

A part of Christina's brain had been destroyed that yokes the eyes so they can function and see. Since the accident, Christina's eyes remained in an unyoked position with each eyeball stuck as though staring at the outer extremity. Her eyelids were always closed or in a half-mast position. Only the whites of her eyes were revealed with her pupils barely visible at the sides. Now we watched in wonder as Christina's gorgeous blue eyes slid from the outer extremity to snap into position front and center.

Then she looked at me.

"Mama, what happened to me? Where am I?" she mouthed. No sound came from her lips due to the tracheotomy, but the words formed by her lips reverberated throughout my entire being.

I burst into tears as the nurse ran out of the room, frightened and shouting for the head nurse.

"She's awake! Christina Varallo is awake!"

She knew this was impossible, but it was indeed happening. Everyone had told us Christina would never wake up. And even if she did, they had warned, she wouldn't know what planet she was on because her brain damage was too extensive. Doctors told us that she would never be coherent and that all speech and cognitive ability were probably lost to her. Yet here she was, mouthing the words, "Mama, what happened? Where am I?"

It just so happened that all the physicians who were directors of the various areas of coma-care specialization were in our wing of the hospital at that moment. They heard the commotion when the nurse ran out of our room, motioning wildly to them and screaming, "Christina Varallo is awake and trying to talk!"

Everyone started running down the hall, shouting,

"Impossible!"

"She can't be talking! That can't be!"

Rushing into the room, the doctors swept me aside, crowding tightly around her bed. The first doctor who reached Christina was the Director of Neurological Psychiatry.

"Christina," he said, "I'm going to ask you a few questions."

She looked directly at him.

"Look at how alert she is," someone muttered.

"She appears to acknowledge what he's saying," another replied.

"If you can understand me," he continued, "if you are hearing me, I want you to close your eyes and keep them closed until I tell you to open them."

I thought, *My goodness, not that! It's taken us more than two months to get those eyes opened! Don't ask her to do that of all things!*

She gave him a quizzical little expression that I recognized very well. Then instantly, she snapped her eyes shut. Finally, he said, "Christina, open your eyes now." And she did, looking straight at him. He started crying. Everyone gasped at once. The room was electrified.

"Impossible!" someone exclaimed.

The Awakening

For months, Christina had been comatose in a persistent vegetative state. But now, suddenly, she was awakening at full steam, with her senses and mental faculties in full operation. By all accounts, it was unbelievable.

Before an audience of medical specialists, the Healer stretched forth His hand. While the doctors stood baffled, seeing but still not believing, the God for whom all things are possible displayed His mighty power. Everyone was in an uproar with the excitement of Christina's awakening.

By this time, Dr. Bonke had been notified and was in the room, joining the other doctors in their questions and tests of Christina's alertness and agility.

"Christina, raise your right leg."

She did.

"Christina, would you please lift your left arm?"

She did.

Christina was looking around the room, wondering what on earth was going on. I was at the very back of the gathering crowd, thinking, *Hello? May I have a chance to hold my own child, please?*

In the middle of all this activity, the phone rang. It was Christina's then boyfriend, Rob, who had stayed with her through all of this. Every day he would call, and we would hold the phone to her ear so he could tell Christina he loved her. When I motioned to Dr. Bonke and told her who was on the line, she took the receiver and briefly spoke to Rob. Then she said, "Christina, someone wants to speak to you," and held the phone to Christina's ear.

As soon as Christina heard her boyfriend's voice, she started to cry and say his name, although of course he couldn't hear her.

But Dr. Bonke could read Christina's lips as she mouthed words and tried to say Rob's name. It was a test of recognition. It was evident immediately: Christina had a memory!

Because of her tracheotomy, the only sound Christina could make was a kissing sound, which she did into the phone. When we told Rob that Christina was fully awake and that the sound he heard was her sending him kisses, he just lost it. We all did. It was too wonderful.

As soon as we saw Christina's response to Rob, we called Nick so she could send him kisses as well. When I took the phone to speak with Nick, all we could manage to speak was each other's names, "Oh, my God," and then we both just sobbed. That said it all. Before leaving the room, Dr. Bonke asked me, "What happened in this room?" I said, "Nothing, only what we have believed for." And she said, "Well, Mama, you have your daughter back. You have your miracle!" But the battle wasn't over.

A Counter Attack

That night nurses came in to suction Christina. One was new. The other nurse, who was named Cheryl, had been assigned to Christina since our arrival. Cheryl is a remarkable woman about Christina's age. She had become—and remains to this day—a dear friend.

There was a sign above Christina's bed which read, "Do not leave the room for ten minutes after patient is suctioned." This message was a crucial alert for the respiratory team to wait until it was certain that Christina didn't have a bronchial attack after the procedure. No one was willing to take any chances, so they made it a point to linger after each treatment.

On that particular evening, I was sure that everything was going to be just fine in light of what God had spoken to my heart that morning. Everything seemed to go well. The team waited for ten minutes, and all was still fine, so they left. But ten minutes later, the alarms on the oxygen monitor suddenly went off in a startling explosion of sound. Somehow it was happening again—Christina was in distress. Only this time, she wasn't comatose. She was fully alert and very aware of the fact that her bronchial tubes were shut down and she was suffocating from lack of oxygen.

Christina's eyes were wide in shock as her fingers grabbed wildly in the air, motioning to us the terror of her struggle to take in air. Cheryl grabbed the Ambu bag on the wall and started working on Christina, who was turning blue by that time. Cheryl and the other nurse moved as quickly as they could to attach all the additional oxygen, but they were hindered by Christina's flailing arms. My daughter was panicking, trapped with no control over what was happening to her own ability to breathe. Because her bronchial tubes had shut down on their own, she could not simply make them open. Finally, the two nurses succeeded in their efforts to attach the additional oxygen. However, Christina's oxygen level was dropping faster than it ever had before.

"Go get help!" Cheryl shouted to the other nurse, who was becoming hysterical and kept repeating over and over, "What are we going to do? What are we going to do?"

"I'll go get help," I said.

"No," Cheryl said, firmly taking charge, "you stay here. Ruth, you go and get help."

"I can't," she replied, frozen with fear. "I can't, I can't!"

"Ruth!" Cheryl demanded, "I've GOT to have help!"

As if on cue, the phone rang. I picked it up to find Nick on the line.

"Nicky!" I screamed. "We're in trouble! Just a minute." I dropped the phone and rushed to the foot of the bed. Everyone was shouting something at each other or at Christina, telling her to breathe, which she couldn't do, or calling out for help. Christina's eyes were beginning to roll backward. She was losing her fight for air.

On the inside, I heard the voice of the Holy One say, "I told you, speak to this condition and tell it to be gone!"

I rushed up and put my hand on Christina's chest and screamed at the top of my lungs, "I say BREATHE in the name of Jesus! Oxygen, be! Bronchial tubes, be open! Bronchial spasms, be gone!"

Through the phone dangling off the hook, Nick was shouting, "Mary Fran! Mary Frances!" He probably thought I had lost my mind. Everyone was shouting, and I was screaming the loudest above all the rest.

Then suddenly, Christina gasped, and her airway cleared. Her oxygen levels eventually rose to normal, and she maintained it at a hundred percent and remained that way till the day they removed the trachea, and there was never again a bronchial spasm. I was trembling at the thought of what could have happened if we had all walked out earlier, just because it looked as though everything was fine.

I realized that the Holy Spirit had alerted me to speak to the bronchial situation with Christina not because it was to be dealt with as I had with the fever, when God showed it to me as a mountain to be cast into the sea. This time, I was alerted to speak to the situation *when* it occurred, not necessarily to prevent it. It is so vital to listen closely to the Holy Spirit and to yield to His guidance in the details of all things. So often we want to do in one situation what proved successful in an earlier situation; then we're disappointed when we don't have the same results. How do we know the difference? By keeping our ear closely tuned to His voice and obeying

Him without question—every time. The Holy Spirit will always lead us to victory and help us sail through any storm if we pay attention when He speaks and obey without delay.

Hath God Said It? Shall He Not Do It?

Nick caught the very first flight he could and arrived early the next day. When he entered the room and saw Christina, he stopped short—absolutely speechless. He could barely believe it had happened in the less than forty-eight hours since he had last seen her. She was totally transformed.

Christina was still hooked up to all the machines, but she followed Nick with her eyes as he made his way around and through the web of wires and tubes attached to her. As he drew closer, Christina kept smiling, her eyes glistening with anticipation. She pursed her lips to make the "smack, smack" sound of kisses toward him as she waited for him to come to her.

When Nick reached Christina, he kissed her and held her in his arms as best he could with all her attachments. Nick touched her face as Christina lifted her hand to reach for his. Sitting there watching them together, I was overcome with emotion and awe to see Nick holding the one thing he had longed for above all else, the one thing that less than forty-eight hours before he thought might never be. But God had given it to him, his daughter. The beauty of that moment was so precious; it was almost sacred.

Nick turned toward me. Then he slid around and picked me up and out of the chair. As he stood there holding me in his arms, he looked deeply into my eyes with an expression that spoke volumes, and in a quiet voice brimming with emotion, he said, "Thank you. Thank you...." Then he just held me. No words were necessary. All the relief, gratitude, and love we felt surpassed anything that could possibly be said.

God had done exactly what He said He would do. By His graces and tender mercies, God had restored life and wholeness to our daughter Christina.

There Is a Child in All of Us

There is a child in all of us, even in all our "grownup-ness." There is a child within us even throughout all our life experiences. Despite all our education and all our intellect, there remains a child within our hearts.

It was from that childlike place, during my most difficult time, that I seemed to raise my voice in song or in words of rhyme like a poet. I am definitely not a singer or a poet. But in the most difficult times, I sing or speak out from that place. From that place in my heart where there is yet a trusting child before my Lord, I come with the innocence of a child relying upon a warm, comforting Parent, my Father God.

In the times of anguish and great pain, in the giving of my simple songs or words, He is suddenly there. And there comes a quieting of my soul, a comforting of my heart. His peaceful rest soothes my strained, wearied body.

God will be this to you as well. When you are the most forgotten, the most lonely, the most tired, the child within you can speak out to Him, and *suddenly*, the atmosphere will be consumed with His loving presence as His loving-kindness comes to envelop and rescue you. When was a time recently when you wanted to run to God as a child? How did He show Himself to be your "Father"?

Journal

_____

_____

_____

_____

_____

_____

_____

_____

_____

_____

_____

_____

_____

_____

9

The Other Side

*"The Lord will sustain, refresh, and strengthen him
on his bed of languishing; all his bed You [O Lord]
will turn, change, and transform in his illness."*

PSALM 41:3 AMP

Every moment is an hour and every hour is a day
when you're waiting for God's promise to be
fulfilled. Days can yawn on into weeks. Weeks stretch
into months, while every single day becomes a battle not
to give in to what you hear, feel, or see.

Since you are locked in the weakness of your
humanity, the only thing that will get you through to the

other side of your trial is fellowship with God. It is not the quoting of Scriptures that will transport you through the fires of great testing; it is fellowship with the Father. It is not the making of continual confessions that will grant you safe passage through the storm; it is communion with the Holy One, the precious Holy Spirit of God.

It is a mistake to try to rely upon the Word without the Holy Spirit. If we focus only on the Word, we can enter into a legalistic bondage. If we attempt to focus only on the Spirit, we lose balance, for the Word is our foundation. But we were not created for bondage or to be off balance. God has created and called us into a bond of relationship and fellowship with Him—through the Word and by His Spirit.

The Person of the Holy Spirit makes the Father known to us through the Word. That is how we become acquainted with the Holy Spirit's voice, for He speaks in agreement with the Word. Through the Word of God—be it the written or the living Word (Jesus Christ)—we gain access to the Father by the Spirit. And we learn how to walk out our relationship as sons or daughters of the Father through fellowship with the Holy Spirit

What is the key to endurance? Fellowship. How do you hold on to what you believe when every other visible or reasonable hope is gone? Fellowship. When you know the One who promised, it's not difficult to trust Him to keep His Word.

Fellowship is what teaches and enables us to walk out the realities of our relationship with the Father God. Fellowship and vital communion is the bedrock of our relationship with the Father that secures our connection to Him so we can walk through a miracle and make it safely to the other side. Fellowship is also the lifeline to hold us steady when we are suspended between the peaks of "Amen, I believe I receive" and "Praise God, here it is!"

From the time the Holy Spirit first spoke to me the words *life and wholeness for Christina,* a period of more than two months transpired. On that journey, every day was a unique battle within itself. The awakening of Christina occurred suddenly. But her restoration to wholeness was a long road back and a story unto itself.

She remained in a wheelchair for almost one year afterward, forced to relearn through months of intense therapy what most of us consider elemental tasks, such as how to talk, crawl, or walk. The list of activities that the doctors told Christina would be difficult or impossible for her to accomplish included running, driving a car, living independently, snow skiing, water skiing, and bike riding. Christina has since accomplished all the above activities and more.

Christina also went through a battery of IQ tests. She tested in the 78 percentile of college graduates. Her daddy said she woke up smarter. She also applied and was accepted into the graduate school program of the University of Tennessee and Peabody at Vanderbilt University. Christina's case record is on a computer chip in the medical computer in Denver, Colorado, where cases for which there are no known statistics for such an outcome are kept. We have a big God, and He's not a respecter of persons.

God said "life and wholeness for Christina" when there was seemingly no hope for wholeness and very little hope for her life. God gave her brain and body back to her just as He had spoken. She remained in the hospital for four months, and it was within a year that she walked again. Eighteen months after the accident she returned to work.

Christina now lives in a beautiful apartment in the city and works in the public relations department of a Nashville company. She is very committed and active in her local church and is dating a wonderful young man. At this printing, she is preparing to participate in an upcoming competitive tandem bike race. Christina believes in a miracle-working God.

Sometimes the road to a miracle is short. Sometimes it can be long. What makes the difference? I honestly do not know. But of one thing I am certain, walking in fellowship with the living God will enable you to cross the great divide between tragedy and miraculous deliverance. Because when the storms of life come, as they do to us all, the Person of the Holy Spirit can be trusted to guide you safely through to the other side.

The Varallo family: Dr. Nick Varallo Jr., Mary Frances, Nicholas, and Christina.

You Were Born for This Time in History

The yearning of God's heart is that we might know Him—*really* know Him. The fervent desire of the Holy Spirit is that we would hear Him and obey Him. The Holy Spirit is the Author and the inspiration to the writers of the Holy Scriptures. Everything He does and says is a reflection of the character of the Godhead and of the written Word of God. He ministers to you out of the character of the content of His Word. The Holy One not only wants to minister to you; He also desires to minister *through* you.

Dearest reader, you were born for this particular time in human history. I believe mankind has entered the corridor of the time of the end. Father God planned and purposed that you live at this time. There is much to be done. And there are things that only you can do.

The Lord created you with gifts and anointings for this end-time generation. You can know of these gifts and anointings by the Holy Spirit. He is the One Whom Jesus said is the Spirit of Truth. He will declare and decree those things concerning your life. He will show you the Father and the Son. He will speak to you of Them, and He will teach you Their ways. Jesus said the Holy Spirit will even speak of and show you things to come. He will be with you and reveal the written Word to you. You have only to ask Him, with a prayer such as this:

"Holy Spirit, please help me study the very Word You authored. Help me pray. I know *how* to pray, but I do not know *what* to pray. Help me, please, to know You better."

The Holy Spirit will never intrude. He waits to be asked. Even right now, He waits. Maybe you could say, "Holy Spirit, You know that I really don't know You, but I want to."

And perhaps you will hear Him respond to your heart, *Wonderful! I have been waiting for you. I have much to say to you. I have much to show you. Let us begin...*

As you have been reading this book, what is the Holy Spirit speaking to you? How is He revealing the nature and love of God to you today? What is the Holy Spirit placing in your heart for your future, your plans, your destiny? Make time in your day to listen to His voice and hear His inner leading.

Journal

Journal

10

$\mathcal{D}$

God Wants You Whole

> *"My son, do not forget my law, but let your heart keep my commands; for length of days and long life and peace they will add to you."*

PROVERBS 3:1,2 NKJV

God has divinely crafted a glorious design for your life. It is an awesome, splendid plan born in the heart of God just for *you*. The devil does not want that plan to come to pass. Therefore, he sends sickness, disease, poverty, despair, lack, or destruction in any area of your life that he can.

Satan's darts are launched against your life to challenge the promise of God that ensures the unfolding of your destiny. But mainly, Satan's darts are thrust at you to persuade you to distrust God and to disbelieve His love for you.

From eternity past, before the foundations of the world, our loving Father God had a plan—to walk as one in close fellowship with man. That plan was expressed in perfection through the life of Jesus. The fellowship Jesus enjoyed with the Father is available to us also as sons and daughters of the living God. That communion and fellowship with God, which is marked by our trust and willful obedience to His words, was the very prize Satan sought to steal in the Garden of Eden.

Why is that? Satan wants to steal our allegiance simply because God has set His love upon us. Satan's goal, with every attack, is to make us doubt or disobey God's words in order to draw us away from the fellowship that is to be the very focus and strength of our lives.

Knowing and believing the truth will enable you to hold fast to your divinely ordained destiny and to be assured of your outcome at the very onset of Satan's attacks.

What is the truth that will hold you steady? God loves you. No good thing will He withhold from you. Sickness, disease, and calamity do not come from God. Our Father God wants you whole.

Let God's Words Hold Final Authority in Your Life

It doesn't matter what you may be facing right now—no matter how bleak or final your circumstances may seem—it isn't over until it's over. God's Word alone is the final authority. And when *your* words remain in steadfast agreement with *God's* Word, you seal His will as the final authority in your life and situation.

You don't have to waiver or wonder any longer. What does God want? *God wants you whole.*

Settle that in your heart. Settle that in your mind. Saturate yourself with the supernatural, living words of God until you can see the unseen. Focus on our loving Father of mercies until you can see yourself whole. Lock your soul into the position of believing that God cannot and will not lie to you. Then hold on to His promises.

You may not see your miracle today. You may not see it tomorrow. But if you believe what God has promised; if you continue to speak what He has said; if you will not let go of His words or relinquish your trust in Him regardless of what you see or feel, God's promises *will* come to pass in every area of your life.

Satan comes to steal, kill, and destroy. But Jesus has come to give you life abundant, life eternal, life everlasting. The reason Jesus gave you abundant, overflowing life is very simple: God wants you blessed. God wants you healed. God wants you prosperous. God wants you delivered. God wants you *whole*—spirit, soul, and body.

If you are not sure of what God has promised you, I encourage you to find out what He said belongs to you. The Word of God is full of rich and specific declarations of the Father's will concerning you. The more of His Word you know, the more convinced of His will you become. The more time you spend with Him in fellowship, the more convinced you will become of His love for you, and trusting Him will become your automatic response. But the fact of the matter is this: All it takes is one word of God set aflame by faith in your heart to totally, completely, and magnificently transform your life and set you free!

I encourage you to search the Scriptures and allow the Holy Spirit to speak to your heart the words that will lead you from death to life in your particular situation. On the following pages, I have included some Scriptures to help strengthen your trust and confidence in our wonderful, healing Jesus.

As you read His words, may His voice become clearer and more real to you than the voices of sickness, pain, poverty, destruction, or despair. These voices, saturated with doubt and fear, call out to you to believe what you see, to accept circumstances, to abandon the hope that your situation will ever change, and to relinquish your right to divine intervention.

But I challenge you: Turn your ear to the Eternal One Whose words cannot fail. Lift your eyes to see your salvation forever settled in Jesus—your Healer—the One Who took away your reproach and bore your sickness and pain. And as you stand still, beholding *Him* with a steadfast, absorbing gaze—you shall be changed.

Suddenly.

Now Let Me Help You...

You've read how I faced one of the greatest difficulties of my life. Perhaps you, too, are facing a great trial of your faith right now. May I pray with you?

My Father, the reader and I come to you by the blood of Jesus and in the name of Jesus—He Who is Your only begotten Son.

My Father, I believe that the reader will receive from Your heart that which he or she must have by the power and the presence of the most Holy Spirit. Thank You, my Father. In Jesus' name, amen.

What difficulties have you been facing? As you've seen from my story, God can deliver you from all of them. Begin to thank God for His deliverance and victory. Begin to see the light at the end of the tunnel. Put your faith in God's love and desire to see you come out of those difficulties victorious! Take some time to reflect on where you are now, and where you **know** God is going to take you.

Journal

11

Healing Scriptures

*"[God's words] are life to those who find them, healing and
health to all their flesh."*

PROVERBS 4:22 AMP

You cannot have confidence in God's willingness to
move in your behalf until you know God's thoughts
concerning you. And you will never know God's thoughts
or comprehend His will apart from His Word.

Throughout the Scriptures, under both the old and
the new covenants, God the Father repeatedly expressed
that it is His will for all to be healed. Following are some

Scriptures that present the heart of our loving Father toward you. I encourage you to fellowship with Him and receive His words into your spirit. God's words are spirit and they are life. And they will transform you entirely—spirit, soul, and body—and make you whole.

Old Testament Promises

Worship the Lord your God, and his blessing will be on your food and water. I will take away sickness from among you, and none will miscarry or be barren in your land. I will give you a full life span.

EXODUS 23:25,26 NIV

God is not a man, that he should lie, nor a son of man, that he should change his mind. Does he speak and then not act? Does he promise and not fulfill?

NUMBERS 23:19 NIV

For the Eternal's eyes dart here and there over the whole world, as he exerts his power on behalf of those who are devoted to him.

2 CHRONICLES 16:9 MOFFATT

So the Lord heard Hezekiah and healed the people.

2 Chronicles 30:20 nas

Thou shalt come to thy grave in a full age, like as a shock of corn cometh in in his season.

Job 5:26

Touching the Almighty...he is excellent in power, and in judgment, and in plenty of justice: he will not afflict.

Job 37:23

O Lord my God, I called to you for help and you healed me.

Psalm 30:2 niv

Many are the afflictions of the righteous: but the Lord delivereth him out of them all.

Psalm 34:19

The Lord will sustain, refresh, and strengthen him on his bed of languishing; all his bed You [O Lord] will turn, change, and transform in his illness.

Psalm 41:3 amp

Because he has set his love upon Me, therefore will I deliver him; I will set him on high, because he knows and understands My name [has a personal knowledge of My mercy, love, and kindness—trusts and relies on me, knowing I will never forsake him, no, never].

He shall call upon Me, and I will answer him; I will be with him in trouble, I will deliver him and honor him.

With long life will I satisfy him and show him My salvation.

PSALM 91:14-16 AMP

Bless (affectionately, gratefully praise) the Lord, O my soul, and forget not [one of] all His benefits—Who forgives [every one of] all your iniquities, Who heals [each one of] all your diseases.

PSALM 103:2,3 AMP

He sent forth his word and healed them; he rescued them from the grave.

PSALM 107:20 NIV

He heals the brokenhearted and binds up their wounds [curing their pains and their sorrows].

PSALM 147:3 AMP

My son, do not forget my law, but let your heart keep my commands; for length of days and long life and peace they will add to you.

PROVERBS 3:1,2 NKJV

Do not be wise in your own eyes; fear the Lord and shun evil. This will bring health to your body and nourishment to your bones.

PROVERBS 3:7,8 NIV

My son, attend to my words; consent and submit to my sayings. Let them not depart from your sight; keep them in the center of your heart. For they are life to those who find them, healing and health to all their flesh.

PROVERBS 4:20-22 AMP

He giveth power to the faint; and to them that have no might he increaseth strength.

ISAIAH 40:29

But they that wait upon the Lord shall renew their strength; they shall mount up with wings as eagles; they shall run, and not be weary; and they shall walk, and not faint.

ISAIAH 40:31

Fear thou not; for I am with thee: be not dismayed; for I am thy God: I will strengthen thee; yea, I will help thee; yea, I will uphold thee with the right hand of my righteousness.

ISAIAH 41:10

So shall my word be that goeth forth out of my mouth: it shall not return unto me void, but it shall accomplish that which I please, and it shall prosper in the thing whereto I sent it.

ISAIAH 55:11

Then shall your light break forth like the morning, and your healing (your restoration and the power of a new life) shall spring forth speedily; your righteousness (your rightness, your

*justice, and your right relationship with God) shall go before
you [conducting you to peace and prosperity], and the glory
of the Lord shall be your rear guard.*

ISAIAH 58:8 AMP

*Heal me, O Lord, and I will be healed; save me and I will be
saved, for You are my praise.*

JEREMIAH 17:14 NAS

For I am the Lord, I change not.

MALACHI 3:6

*But unto you who revere and worshipfully fear My name shall
the Sun of Righteousness arise with healing in His wings and
His beams, and you shall go forth and gambol like calves
[released] from the stall and leap for joy.*

MALACHI 4:2 AMP

New Testament Promises

*Jesus went throughout Galilee, teaching in their synagogues,
preaching the good news of the kingdom, and healing every
disease and sickness among the people.*

218

News about him spread all over Syria, and people brought to him all who were ill with various diseases, those suffering severe pain, the demon-possessed, those having seizures, and the paralyzed, and he healed them.

Matthew 4:23,24 niv

And a leper came to Him, and throwing himself at His feet, said,

"Sir, if only you are willing you are able to cleanse me." So Jesus put out His hand and touched him, and said, "I am willing: be cleansed." Instantly he was cleansed from his leprosy.

Matthew 8:2,3 Weymouth

And when Jesus was entered into Capernaum, there came unto him a centurion, beseeching him, and saying, Lord, my servant lieth at home sick of the palsy, grievously tormented.

And Jesus saith unto him, I will come and heal him.

The centurion answered and said, Lord, I am not worthy that thou shouldest come under my roof: but speak the word only, and my servant shall be healed. For I am a man under authority, having soldiers under me: and I say to this man, Go, and he goeth; and to another, Come, and he cometh; and to my servant, Do this, and he doeth it.

219

When Jesus heard it, he marvelled, and said to them that followed, Verily I say unto you, I have not found so great faith, no, not in Israel.

And Jesus said unto the centurion, Go thy way; and as thou hast believed, so be it done unto thee. And his servant was healed in the selfsame hour.

MATTHEW 8:5-10,13

And when Jesus went into Peter's house, He saw his mother-in-law lying ill with a fever.

He touched her hand and the fever left her; and she got up and began waiting on Him.

When evening came, they brought to Him many who were under the power of demons, and He drove out the spirits with a word and restored to health all who were sick.

And thus He fulfilled what was spoken by the prophet Isaiah, He Himself took [in order to carry away] our weaknesses and infirmities and bore away our diseases.

MATTHEW 8:14-17 AMP

And a woman who had a hemorrhage for twelve years came up and touched the tassel on His coat.

For she kept saying to herself, "If I can only touch His coat, I will get well."

And Jesus, on turning and seeing her, said, "Cheer up, my daughter! Your faith has cured you." And from that moment the woman was well.

MATTHEW 9:20-22 WILLIAMS

And when he had called unto him his twelve disciples, he gave them power against unclean spirits, to cast them out, and to heal all manner of sickness and all manner of disease.

MATTHEW 10:1

And as ye go, preach, saying, The kingdom of heaven is at hand. Heal the sick, cleanse the lepers, raise the dead, cast out devils: freely ye have received, freely give.

MATTHEW 10:7,8

But when Jesus knew it, he withdrew himself from thence: and great multitudes followed him, and he healed them all.

MATTHEW 12:15

When Jesus heard what had happened, he withdrew by boat privately to a solitary place. Hearing of this, the crowds followed him on foot from the towns. When Jesus landed and saw a large crowd, he had compassion on them and healed their sick.

MATTHEW 14:13,14 NIV

Jesus left there and went along the Sea of Galilee. Then he went up on a mountainside and sat down. Great crowds came to him, bringing the lame, the blind, the crippled, the mute and many others, and laid them at his feet; and he healed them. The people were amazed when they saw the mute speaking, the crippled made well, the lame walking and the blind seeing. And they praised the God of Israel.

MATTHEW 15:29-31 NIV

Again I tell you, if two of you on earth agree (harmonize together, make a symphony together) about whatever [anything and everything] they may ask, it will come to pass and be done for them by My Father in heaven.

MATTHEW 18:19 AMP

The blind and the lame came to him at the temple, and he healed them.

MATTHEW 21:14 NIV

When Jesus had again crossed over by boat to the other side of the lake, a large crowd gathered around him while he was by the lake. Then one of the synagogue rulers, named Jairus, came there. Seeing Jesus, he fell at his feet and pleaded earnestly with him, "My little daughter is dying. Please come and put your hands on her so that she will be healed and live." So Jesus went with him.

A large crowd followed and pressed around him. And a woman was there who had been subject to bleeding for twelve years. She had suffered a great deal under the care of many doctors and had spent all she had, yet instead of getting better she grew worse. When she heard about Jesus, she came up behind him in the crowd and touched his cloak, because she thought, "If I just touch his clothes, I will be healed." Immediately her bleeding stopped and she felt in her body that she was freed from her suffering.

At once Jesus realized that power had gone out from him. He turned around in the crowd and asked, "Who touched my clothes?"

"You see the people crowding against you," his disciples answered, "and yet you can ask, 'Who touched me?'"

But Jesus kept looking around to see who had done it. Then the woman, knowing what had happened to her, came and fell at his feet and, trembling with fear, told him the whole truth. He said to her, "Daughter, your faith has healed you. Go in peace and be freed from your suffering."

While Jesus was still speaking, some men came from the house of Jairus, the synagogue ruler. "Your daughter is dead," they said. "Why bother the teacher any more?"

Ignoring what they said, Jesus told the synagogue ruler, "Don't be afraid; just believe."

He did not let anyone follow him except Peter, James and John the brother of James. When they came to the home of the synagogue ruler, Jesus saw a commotion, with people crying and wailing loudly. He went in and said to them, "Why all this commotion and wailing? The child is not dead but asleep." But they laughed at him.

After he put them all out, he took the child's father and mother and the disciples who were with him, and went in where the child was. He took her by the hand and said to her, "Talitha koum!" (which means, "Little girl, I say to you, get up!"). Immediately the girl stood up and walked around (she was twelve years old). At this they were completely astonished. He gave strict orders not to let anyone know about this, and told them to give her something to eat.

MARK 5:21-43 NIV

He could not do any mighty deeds there, except that He put His hands on a few ailing people and cured them.

And He wondered at their lack of faith in Him.

MARK 6:5,6 WILLIAMS

For verily I say unto you, That whosoever shall say unto this mountain, Be thou removed, and be thou cast into the sea; and shall not doubt in his heart, but shall believe that those things which he saith shall come to pass; he shall have whatsoever he saith.

Therefore I say unto you, What things soever ye desire, when ye pray, believe that ye receive them, and ye shall have them.

MARK 11:23,24

And he said unto them, Go ye into all the world, and preach the gospel to every creature.

He that believeth and is baptized shall be saved; but he that believeth not shall be damned.

And these signs shall follow them that believe; In my name shall they cast out devils; they shall speak with new tongues; they shall take up serpents; and if they drink any deadly thing, it shall not hurt them; they shall lay hands on the sick, and they shall recover.

So then after the Lord had spoken unto them, he was received up into heaven, and sat on the right hand of God.

And they went forth, and preached every where, the Lord working with them, and confirming the word with signs following. Amen.

MARK 16:15-20

And he came to Nazareth, where he had been brought up: and, as his custom was, he went into the synagogue on the sabbath day, and stood up for to read.

And there was delivered unto him the book of the prophet Esaias. And when he had opened the book, he found the place where it was written,

The Spirit of the Lord is upon me, because he hath anointed me to preach the gospel to the poor; he hath sent me to heal *the brokenhearted, to preach deliverance to the captives, and recovering of sight to the blind, to set at liberty them that are bruised, to preach the acceptable year of the Lord.*

And he closed the book, and he gave it again to the minister, and sat down. And the eyes of all them that were in the synagogue were fastened on him.

And he began to say unto them, This day is this scripture fulfilled in your ears.

LUKE 4:16-21

When the sun was setting, the people brought to Jesus all who had various kinds of sickness, and laying his hands on each one, he healed them.

LUKE 4:40 NIV

And it came to pass also on another sabbath, that he entered into the synagogue and taught: and there was a man whose right hand was withered.

And the scribes and Pharisees watched him, whether he would heal on the sabbath day; that they might find an accusation against him.

But he knew their thoughts, and said to the man which had the withered hand, Rise up, and stand forth in the midst. And he arose and stood forth.

Then said Jesus unto them, I will ask you one thing; Is it lawful on the sabbath days to do good, or to do evil? to save life, or to destroy it?

And looking round about upon them all, he said unto the man, Stretch forth thy hand. And he did so: and his hand was restored whole as the other.

LUKE 6:6-10

And it came to pass, as he went to Jerusalem, that he passed through the midst of Samaria and Galilee.

And as he entered into a certain village, there met him ten men that were lepers, which stood afar off: And they lifted up their voices, and said, Jesus, Master, have mercy on us.

And when he saw them, he said unto them, Go shew yourselves unto the priests. And it came to pass, that, as they went, they were cleansed.

And one of them, when he saw that he was healed, turned back, and with a loud voice glorified God, and fell down on his face at his feet, giving him thanks: and he was a Samaritan.

And Jesus answering said, Were there not ten cleansed? but where are the nine?

There are not found that returned to give glory to God, save this stranger. And he said unto him, Arise, go thy way: thy faith hath made thee whole.

LUKE 17:11-19

The thief cometh not, but for to steal, and to kill, and to destroy: I am come that they might have life, and that they might have it more abundantly.

JOHN 10:10

And whatsoever ye shall ask in my name, that will I do, that the Father may be glorified in the Son. If ye shall ask any thing in my name, I will do it.

JOHN 14:13,14

If you remain in me and my words remain in you, ask whatever you wish, and it will be given you.

JOHN 15:7 NIV

There came also a multitude out of the cities round about unto Jerusalem, bringing sick folks, and them which were vexed with unclean spirits: and they were healed every one.

ACTS 5:16

And there he found a certain man named Aeneas, which had kept his bed eight years, and was sick of the palsy. And Peter said unto him, Aeneas, Jesus Christ maketh thee whole: arise, and make thy bed. And he arose immediately.

ACTS 9:33,34

How God anointed Jesus of Nazareth with the Holy Ghost and with power: who went about doing good, and healing all that were oppressed of the devil; for God was with him.

ACTS 10:38

And God wrought special miracles by the hands of Paul:

So that from his body were brought unto the sick handkerchiefs or aprons, and the diseases departed from them, and the evil spirits went out of them.

ACTS 19:11,12

And being not weak in faith, he considered not his own body now dead, when he was about an hundred years old, neither yet the deadness of Sara's womb:

He staggered not at the promise of God through unbelief; but was strong in faith, giving glory to God;

And being fully persuaded that, what he had promised, he was able also to perform.

ROMANS 4:19-21

Since He did not spare His own son but gave Him up for us all, will he not with Him graciously give us everything else?

ROMANS 8:32 WILLIAMS

But if the Spirit of Him who raised Jesus from the dead dwells in you, He who raised Christ from the dead will also give life to your mortal bodies through His Spirit who dwells in you.

ROMANS 8:11 NKJV

Inasmuch then as we have a great High Priest Who has [already] ascended and passed through the heavens, Jesus the Son of God, let us hold fast our confession [of faith in Him].

For we do not have a High Priest Who is unable to understand and sympathize and have a shared feeling with our weaknesses and infirmities and liability to the assaults of temptation, but One Who has been tempted in every respect as we are, yet without sinning.

Let us then fearlessly and confidently and boldly draw near to the throne of grace (the throne of God's unmerited favor to us sinners), that we may receive mercy [for our failures] and find grace to help in good time for every need [appropriate help and well-timed help, coming just when we need it].

HEBREWS 4:14-16 AMP

Let us hold fast the profession of our faith without wavering; (for he is faithful that promised).

HEBREWS 10:23

Now do not drop that confidence of yours; it carries with it a rich hope of reward.

Steady patience is what you need, so that after doing the will of God you may receive what you were promised.

HEBREWS 10:35,36 MOFFATT

Now faith is a well-grounded assurance of that for which we hope, and a conviction of the reality of things which we do not see.

HEBREWS 11:1 WEYMOUTH

Jesus Christ is the same yesterday and today and forever.

HEBREWS 13:8 NAS

Is anyone sick among you? He should call on the elders of the church, and they should pray over him, and anoint him with oil in the name of the Lord,

and the prayer that is offered in faith will save the sick man; the Lord will raise him to health, and if he has committed sins, he will be forgiven.

So practice confessing your sins to one another, and praying for one another, that you may be cured. An upright man's prayer, when it keeps at work, is very powerful.

JAMES 5:14-16 WILLIAMS

He personally bore our sins in His [own] body on the tree [as on an altar and offered Himself on it], that we might die

231

(cease to exist) to sin and live to righteousness. By His wounds you have been healed.

1 PETER 2:24 AMP

And this is the confidence (the assurance, the privilege of boldness) which we have in Him: [we are sure] that if we ask anything (make any request) according to His will (in agreement with His own plan), He listens to and hears us.

And if (since) we [positively] know that He listens to us in whatever we ask, we also know [with settled and absolute knowledge] that we have [granted us as our present possessions] the requests made of Him.

1 JOHN 5:14,15 AMP

Beloved, I pray that you may prosper in every way and [that your body] may keep well, even as [I know] your soul keeps well and prospers.

3 JOHN 2 AMP

Journal

Journal

Diary of My Miracle

The need in my life:

_____

_____

_____

_____

_____

_____

_____

_____

_____

_____

_____

_____

_____

_____

Journal

Diary of My Miracle

The foundation (Word) of my faith:

_____

_____

_____

_____

_____

_____

_____

_____

_____

_____

_____

_____

_____

_____

_____

Journal

Diary of My Miracle

The date I believed that I received:

_____

_____

_____

_____

_____

_____

_____

_____

_____

_____

_____

_____

_____

_____

_____

_____

Journal

Diary of My Miracle

The date the manifestation came:

_____

_____

_____

_____

_____

_____

_____

_____

_____

_____

_____

_____

_____

_____

Journal

_____

_____

_____

_____

_____

_____

_____

_____

_____

_____

_____

_____

_____

_____

_____

_____

Journal

Prayer of Salvation

A born-again, committed relationship with God is the key to the victorious life. Jesus, the Son of God, laid down His life and rose again so that we could spend eternity with Him in heaven and experience His absolute best on earth. The Bible says, *"For God so loved the world, that he gave his only begotten Son, that whosoever believeth in him should not perish, but have everlasting life"* (John 3:16).

It is the will of God that everyone receives eternal salvation. The way to receive this salvation is to call upon the name of Jesus and confess Him as your Lord. The Bible says, *"That if thou shalt confess with thy mouth the Lord Jesus, and shalt believe in thine heart that God hath raised him from the dead, thou shalt be saved. For whosoever shall call upon the name of the Lord shall be saved"* (Romans 10:9,13).

Jesus has given salvation, healing, and countless benefits to all who call upon His name. These benefits can be yours if you receive Him into your heart by praying this prayer:

Father,

I come to You right now as a sinner. Right now, I choose to turn away from sin, and I ask You to cleanse me of all unrighteousness. I believe that Your Son, Jesus, died on the cross to take away my sins. I also believe that He rose again from the dead so that I may be justified and made righteous through faith in Him. I call upon the name of Jesus Christ for salvation. I want Him to be the Savior and Lord of my life. Jesus, I choose to follow You, and I ask that You fill me with the power of the Holy Spirit. I declare right now that I am a born-again child of God. I am free from sin and full of the righteousness of God. I am saved in Jesus' name, Amen.

If you have prayed this prayer to receive Jesus Christ into your life, we would like to hear from you. Please write us at the following address:

Harrison House
P.O. Box 35035
Tulsa, Oklahoma 74153

References

Capps, Charles. *God's Creative Power for Healing*. Tulsa: Harrison House Publishing, 1991.

The Amplified Bible (AMP), *Old Testament*. Copyright © 1965, 1987 by Zondervan Corporation, Grand Rapids, Michigan. *The Amplified Bible* (AMP), *New Testament*. Copyright © 1958, 1987 by the Lockman Foundation, La Habra, California. Used by permission.

The Bible. A New Testament (MOFFATT). Copyright © 1950, 1952, 1953, 1954 by James A.R. Moffatt. Harper & Row Publishers, Inc., New York, New York.

The Holy Bible: New International Version® (NIV). Copyright © 1973, 1978, 1984 by International Bible Society. Used by permission of Zondervan Publishing House. All rights reserved.

New American Standard Bible (NAS). Copyright © by the Lockman Foundation 1960, 1962, 1963, 1968, 1971, 1972, 1973, 1975, 1977. Used by permission.

The New King James Version (NKJV). Copyright © 1979, 1980, 1982 by Thomas Nelson, Inc. Used by permission.

Weymouth's New Testament in Modern Speech (WEYMOUTH), by Richard Francis Weymouth. Harper & Row Publishers, Inc., New York, New York.

The New Testament: A Private Translation in the Language of the People by Charles B. Williams (WILLIAMS). Copyright © 1937 by Bruce Humphries, Inc. Copyright assigned, 1949 to The Moody Bible Institutes of Chicago.

About the Author

Rev. Mary Frances Varallo has been called by God to carry the message of His love and power throughout the United States as well as to the nations of the world. She ministers to the lost, the sick, and the oppressed in every land, while God confirms His Word with signs and wonders. Rev. Varallo's ministry is unique in that she reaches persons of a wide variety of ages and backgrounds.

Pastors recognize Rev. Varallo as a gifted minister of the gospel who is mightily used to minister salvation, healing, and restoration. The gifts of the Holy Spirit flow during her meetings and crusades in freshness and power. Rev. Varallo presents a challenge to the body of Christ, stirring in believers a fervent hunger for the things of God, encouraging them to take their place in the local church. Rev. Bill McRay, Senior Pastor of Victory Fellowship Church in Nashville, Tennessee, says of Rev. Varallo, "Wherever she ministers, God shows up in all His power and glory to bless the people."

In January 2001, Rev. Varallo was invited to hold a crusade in Cameroon, a French-Islamic nation on the Ivory Coast. Until that time, it was unheard of for a woman to hold a crusade of this nature. During her meetings there were many notable miracles witnessed including the healing of a well-known soccer player who was on the National Senior Team in West Africa. As a result of these miracles and because Rev. Varallo was the first woman to conduct a crusade in Cameroon, she was invited to visit with the country's Prime Minister and the Admiral of the Navy.

Rev. Varallo is a native of Nashville and has long been active in a leadership capacity for various civic organizations in Tennessee. She attended both Aquinas Junior College and Peabody College, now part of Vanderbilt University, where she pursued a degree in Clinical Psychology. Rev. Varallo has traveled extensively throughout the United States, South America, Eastern and Western Europe, Africa, and Asia. She is a winter sports enthusiast. She and her husband, Dr. Nick Varallo Jr., have two adult children, Nicholas and Christina.

To receive a catalog of tapes by Mary Frances Varallo,
please write to:

Mary Frances Varallo Ministries
P.O. Box 16
Nashville, Tennessee 37203 USA

Varalloworldoutreach.com

or call:
(615) 383-1627

Additional copies of this book
are available from your local bookstore.

Harrison House
Tulsa, Oklahoma 74153

The Harrison House Vision

Proclaiming the truth and the power
Of the Gospel of Jesus Christ
With excellence;

Challenging Christians to
Live victoriously,
Grow spiritually,
Know God intimately.